"*Search* is a book about a fundamental rethinking of our relationships to each other and everything else on the planet. This isn't a book about search engines or any one company; it's a book to help you understand why stores will soon know what you want to buy and why governments will tell us the truth even if they don't know it."
—Peter H. Diamandis, MD, Chairman, XPRIZE Foundation and Singularity University; co-author of the NYT bestseller *Abundance: The Future Is Better Than You Think*

"In his book *Search*, Weitz leads us through a fascinating future where the 'capable web' augments human intellect, search begins to *do*, and where the physical world itself is lit up with web-derived intelligence."
—Adam Cheyer, Siri co-founder

"What do Bluetooth beacons, augmented reality, and predicting the future have in common? Stefan Weitz weaves a compelling tale of what's next in search, and demonstrates his unique talent of distilling this diverse and complicated topic down into something us mere mortals can understand."
—Andy Grignon, co-creator of the iPhone, current CEO of Eightly

"If Stefan Weitz is right—and I think he is—search technology is about to usher our society into a whole new world. If you want to make a difference in the future of tech, read this book."
—Alex Banayan, nation's youngest VC, Alsop Louie Partners and author of forthcoming *The Third Door: How the World's Most Successful People Beat the System and Launched Their Careers*

"Weitz takes us through a whirlwind tour of the future of search—a tour that builds on today's science but imagines the revolutionary possibilities we'll enjoy if we can overcome today's technology and business limitations. A must-read for anyone working in an area that is truly the hinge between humans and machines."

—Daniel Tunkelang, head of Query Understanding at LinkedIn, founder of Endeca Search

"*Search* is more than just an incredible exploration of the future of search, it is an eye-opening look into how search and future technologies will enhance humanity and change everything we do. Read *Search* if you want a glimpse into the future."

—Ben Parr, award-winning journalist, author, entrepreneur, investor

"Weitz artfully frames the pervasive nature of search and the growing importance in changing the way we live and work."

—Joe Marchese, founder of True(x) and co-founder of Reserve.com

"This book captures the essence of why digitization is disrupting all the industries of the world. Media, communications, and information have been disrupted. What's next? Banking, manufacturing, education, government? Read this book and see how digitization will predict your future."

—Tim Draper, founder of Draper Fisher Jurvetson (DFJ)

"Weitz has his finger on the pulse of what the world looks like as we move from search to service. Stepping inside Weitz's mind to understand where search and consumer behavior are going is not only fun but a competitive imperative for any technology professional."

—Gina Bianchini, founder of Ning and Mightybell

"*Search* is an important exploration of how far search has come and how far it has yet to go. There are few questions we can ask that can't be answered today. But the really exciting future of search will come when machines don't just answer the questions but also ask them. Weitz's book allows us to not just imagine, but comprehend, a future in which computers are able to use massive quantities of data to make choices on their own. I, for one, am excited about the future that Weitz describes."

—Dave Hornik, partner at August Capital

"Weitz's vision of search is so near that it's almost obvious, but so stunning that we need him to help us see it. If your livelihood depends on not being blindsided by technology, you must read this."

—Dan Shapiro, former CEO of Google Shopping, founder of Sparkbuy, and creator of Robot Turtles board game

"*Search* is a thought-provoking look into everything that search technology can do for us in the next five, ten, or even twenty years. Weitz has indexed the future, and you'll want to read his results!"

—Dror Berman, managing partner, Innovation Endeavors

"The power unleashed by the technology behind the simple search box has profound impacts on how we live our lives, from how we shop to how we interact with our friends and colleagues. *Search* helps us understand the benefits—and consequences—of this technology disruption in a way that is both hopeful and challenging and highlights the very important choices we will all have to make in the near future."

—Wesley Chan, former Google Executive, partner at Google Ventures

"In the not so distant future, your life will be aided by a personalized search service that runs in the cloud, follows your every move, mines the world's information on your behalf, and notifies you of the answers to your questions before they've even been asked. Stefan Weitz masterfully describes the challenges and opportunities of realizing this future: extending search to map the physical world, to interpret the flood of new sensors and signals, and to model our interests and contexts. *Search* is a prescient view of a life aided by technology and I'm eager to live in the future he describes."

—Pat Kinsel, co-founder of Spindle and current
Venture Partner at Polaris VC

🔍 SEARCH

GREEN
HOUSE
collection

It begins with a book.

A dearly held assumption is challenged. An impossible conversation begins. A vigorous debate ensues, forming friends and foes for a generation. The end of this cycle may be revolution or enlightenment, but look back far enough and there is always a book to thank or to blame.

Created by the founders of Insight Labs, the world's first philanthropic think tank, the Greenhouse Collection is premised on the belief that such exchanges are still possible.

The ideas exhibited in this collection are an invitation to discuss and deconstruct topics of import as they relate to bigger and more complex problems. They are catalysts for further exploration as we endeavor to design and build solutions to the challenges we face today, and those we will face tomorrow, closing the gap between what is and what can be.

SEARCH

HOW THE DATA EXPLOSION
MAKES US SMARTER

STEFAN WEITZ

bibliomotion
books + media

First published by Bibliomotion, Inc.
39 Harvard Street
Brookline, MA 02445
Tel: 617-934-2427
www.bibliomotion.com

Printed in the United States of America

Library of Congress Cataloging-in-Publication Data

Weitz, Stefan.
  Search : how the data explosion makes us smarter / Stefan Weitz.
    pages cm
  Includes bibliographical references and index.
  ISBN 978-1-62956-034-2 (hardcover : alk. paper) — ISBN 978-1-62956-035-9 (ebook) — ISBN 978-1-62956-036-6 (enhanced ebook)
  1. Search engines.   2. Information retrieval.   3. Information storage and retrieval systems.   4. Information behavior.   5. Human-computer interaction.   6. Technological forecasting.   I. Title.
  TK5105.884W46 2014
  025.04—dc23
                                        2014028903

This book is dedicated to the men and women of the United States Armed Forces. It is because of them that I get to do what I do.

CONTENTS

Acknowledgments   xiii

Introduction: Where Is My Flying Car?   xv

1   What Search Will See   1

2   How Search Will Act   37

3   What Search Will Do   59

4   What Search Will Be   83

5   What Search Will Bring Us   103

6   What Holds Search Back: The Technology   115

7   What Holds Search Back: The Business   137

8   A Time to Believe   161

Conclusion: Searching the Future   185

Notes   189

References   191

Index   193

About the Author   199

ACKNOWLEDGMENTS

Writing a book truly takes a village and often left me wondering if I was the idiot of said village. On this topic especially, with the amount of potential things one could potentially include (and thus the many things one could leave out), I was consistently left with the sinking feeling that maybe the answers to the vexing questions regarding the future of search and technology were hiding in plain sight, waiting only for a simple connection I had overlooked that would make everything more clear.

Luckily, I had so many people who helped affirm my curiosity, minimize my concerns that the future of search and its potential were known and solved ponderings, and gave me so much to consider in constructing what might happen when the entire planet is captured in digital and our machines are more aware of their role on it.

Huge thanks is owed to Dr. Eric Horvitz, Dr. Susan Dumais, Dr. Ben Livshits, Dr. Marc Davis, Dr. Adam Cheyer, Dr. Jaime Teevan, Joe Marchese, Adam Macbeth, Anirudh Koul, Shel Israel, and Ramez Naam for inspiration and amazing content.

Chris Schroeder listened and gave me great feedback on writing. Susan Lauzau, my most extraordinary editor, made my words make sense (and knows entirely too much about everything). Adam Sohn gave me the latitude to go spend time away from my real work to write a book (and I wonder if he noticed?).

My daughter Elena – thank you for putting up with daddy's "writing time" when you really wanted to play Labyrinth. To my partner Sarah Elizabeth, thank you for all your moral support and patience in birthing this tome – even when I thought I'd never make the deadline, your positivity duped me into thinking otherwise. To my parents, thank you for getting me my first computer when they still cost as much as a car and letting me spend entirely too much time in the basement learning to program.

Thank you to everyone at Bibliomotion including Erika Heilman and Jill Friedlander; and Howell J. Malham Jr., Jeff Leitner, and Andrew Benedict-Nelson of GreenHouse for both the opportunity and the feedback throughout the process.

Finally, thank you to everyone at Microsoft Bing who are the people who are really bringing so many of these concepts to life in such beautiful ways.

Where Is My Flying Car?

For how long have we been promised robots? For how many decades have we waited for intelligent machines that can drive our cars, empty our trash, take care of our kids, and generally do our bidding? Since we humans first began dreaming of extending our capabilities and leaving the planet—or even our humdrum daily lives—machines have been at the heart of the excursion. And while it may seem as though there is always another advance just over the horizon that will bring this freedom, we are suddenly—almost accidentally—standing at the confluence of a number of innovations. Separately, they are incredible in their scope and impact, but together they promise something far more profound: not just better machines, but better versions of ourselves.

We have spent thousands of years building machines and systems—at first rudimentary ones and then more sophisticated models—that help us think more clearly, accomplish more, and extend our natural human senses and abilities. From the original wheel to pulley and lever systems to stone and iron tools to the slide rule, we humans have long created objects to augment our capacities. And for good reason. Machines in general, and computing systems specifically, are much better at some cognitive functions than we are, including:

• **Rote computation:** The world's fastest supercomputer (as of this writing) can handle thirty-three quadrillion calculations in a second. That's 33,000,000,000,000,000 calculations per second. To put that in perspective, when President Reagan proposed the "Star Wars" defense system in the late 1980s, the part of the system that was designed to float in space, watch for missiles coming from Russia, target them at seventeen thousand miles an hour, and destroy them was said to require a computer that could do sixty million calculations per second.

• **Following complex rules and structures over and over without deviation or failure:** The beauty of machines is that, once you program them with a set of rules, they simply execute the tasks. An operating system like Microsoft's Windows XP contained fifty million lines of code—basically, rules for how the system was to behave. Computers don't get distracted and they don't ask questions. And when the same sorts of problem arise again and again, the ability to apply a known solution that works—and to do so very quickly—is a huge benefit.

• **Spotting patterns across huge amounts of data:** Just as we can program machines to follow a set of rules, we can program them to find correlations and relationships across massive amounts of data. Imagine trying to spot a trend when confronted with billions or even trillions of pieces of information. Human memory storage taps out when the number gets to around seven. While we are good at visual and analog pattern matching—seeing much of the same color in a painting, for example—digital patterns escape us.

• **Storing and retrieving information almost instantly, and nearly without limit:** Our brains hold an unquestionably large amount of data, and we do it in a very elegant way that allows us to see connections between things that machines often miss. However, we also suffer from a finite amount of storage. Even worse, the fidelity with which we recall information degrades, especially over time or when the information is rarely accessed. Machines, barring any mechanical failure, can store a nearly infinite amount of data, reproduce it perfectly billions of times, and retrieve it nearly instantly, no matter how infrequently it is accessed. And unlike a human, who might require seven to ten repetitions before he can memorize a fact and put it in long-term memory, a machine only needs to be told once.

• **Communicating in an efficient, unambiguous way:** Unlike human forms of communication, which have layers of complexity and ambiguity (some would say this is part of our charm), the symbolic languages used by systems have been constructed to represent precise formulations. My girlfriend may tell me she doesn't want to go out, but her words can mask her real wishes. That doesn't happen with a computer; to a computer, up is up, down is down, and false means false. Such a concrete language and the corresponding positive affirmations—which tells us that other systems to which a system has spoken have heard the message—means distributed intelligence can and does occur.

• **Remaining ever vigilant and never requiring a break:** This one is probably most obvious. With the right power (and a way to get rid of the heat generated by the electrical circuitry), a computer never needs to be turned off. Compare that to your author, who desperately needs a break right about now.

But this isn't to say that systems are ready to take over for us meat puppets. There are tasks and problems at which we are better—and will continue to be, potentially for decades or centuries to come—which is a positive sign for both our continued existence and for our advancement as a species. Even if we are able to imbue machines with the ability to "think" and "feel" in the nearish future, there are situations where the relatively slow, egocentric and biased human brain is likely to reign supreme. For example, compared with machines we excel at:

• **Rationalizing our way through a problem we've never seen before.** We humans have an ability to apply mental models and heuristics, developed over millions of years of evolution, to reason our way through a situation even if we have never been in the exact situation before. We see patterns in problems that look vaguely similar to things we have seen previously, and we are able to apply those patterns to the current situation. Even something as simple as a Walk/Don't Walk sign at a crosswalk can foul up a machine if the machine is programmed to read words but the sign uses little red and green people symbols instead. For humans, however, understanding the sign's meaning is a simple task.

• **Learning without being told how and learning what is relevant or exciting on our own.** Humans are able to build knowledge over time without explicit instruction. Young children, for example, learn basics (like walking or recognizing mom and dad) through trial and error without being explicitly taught.

• **Understanding and manipulating our physical environment even if it is unfamiliar.** If you put a human in a hotel room where he has never been, he will easily navigate the room, find the bathroom, and use the coffee maker. This flexible operation is something machines today aren't capable of.

- **Empathy, creativity, and relating to other humans.** The softer side of humanity is still an area where we excel over machines. While there have been advances in imbuing machines with the ability to read human emotions, think independently, and emulate human interactions, they are still pale shadows of the real thing.

What is exciting to me, though, is viewing the power of humans and machines not as an "either/or" but as an "and." What we need is a *hinge* that can join together the best parts of machines and the best parts of humans. We need a metaphorical version of the corpus callosum, the bundle of neural fibers that is located at the center of the brain and connects the two hemispheres. The corpus callosum facilitates interhemispheric communication, allowing, among other things, the logical left brain and emotive right brain to work together to accomplish tasks each might not be able to perform on its own.

I contend that this hinge between human and machine is *search*. It's not the search you know today, and likely not even the search that the big technology companies are currently building—but it's the search that comes into view when we think about it less as a tool for finding pages on the web and more as a group of functions that can be deployed to make us smarter, happier, and better connected in our real-world lives.

To date, search has solved only a small portion of this challenge. In fact, it's likely that the earliest search builders didn't even know this "hinge" was the challenge they were trying to solve. They were mostly concerned with finding a page on the World Wide Web that had one or more of the words entered into a query box. That is not to diminish the remarkable technology that allows us to retrieve one document out of a hundred billion in mere milliseconds based on a couple of words. But, as we will see in the coming chapters, the world around us is increasingly digitized, meaning that everything from the complete characteristics of a Crate and Barrel Gibson coffee table to my complete history of movement across the globe is being captured and stored in computing systems. The possible applications of this advance are profound, but so are the implications if we look at the power of search—especially if we begin to realize it is not a one-size-fits-all tool and every query a nail, but rather that search is a set of tools that can helpfully and aggressively expand our human potential.

The Shape of Things to Come

In my day job, I'm a senior director in search at Microsoft's Bing—I'm one of the many people who works to promote and improve technologies for our search engine. I've been there since the beginning and have been so lucky to be a part of one of the most complex start-up efforts I could have imagined.

In December 2013, I got a call asking me if I would like to write a book about search. I thought, sure—why not? I was planning on traveling to fourteen cities around the world for already scheduled talks and meetings. I was launching a number of new products at Microsoft. And I was just getting off caffeine. I am obviously somewhat unbalanced.

But it was important to me to write my thoughts about what we're facing when every device, every object that surrounds us, and every person is connected and we have systems that can discern patterns among the noise. Search has great power to alert us to things we don't even know we need to know, and to generally enable us to be better versions of ourselves. I see a golden age of digitization coming, when every person, place, and thing is described in digital form. When that age arrives, our human abilities will be enhanced, allowing us to make better decisions and manipulate our physical world with little more than a thought, and ultimately we will become happier as our systems offload intellectual flotsam from our crowded minds. When I speak about my work and my vision for the future of search at dinner parties or during talks at conferences, people invariably become excited about the possibilities. It isn't until we get into the bowels of what it truly means to be hyper-connected, analyzed, and guided by our technology that I get more than a few raised eyebrows.

Tech is a tight-knit industry, and I also have many friends at Google, usually named as our chief competitor. And while I don't have any specific knowledge of what my compatriots are working on in Mountain View, over dinner I get to hear what they think about and about the problems both Bing and Google are looking to solve.

What follows in this book is not a product plan or a commitment by Bing or Microsoft or any other company to build this future of search. Indeed, many of the concepts are controversial and rife with regulatory challenges. In some cases, society simply may not be ready for a world of hyperconnectedness and the transparency that follows. Instead, this is a book about the possible shape of things to come written by someone who lives every day in the depths of the Internet, talks every year with engineers and tech experts at hundreds of companies and with academics who are advancing the state of the art, and generally believes in the power of technology to build a freer and happier society.

Humans + Machines = Love

We humans have always looked for ways to capture what we are seeing in the real world so that it can be saved, passed on, and learned from. Cave drawings, journals, essays, photographs, recordings, videos—these traces enable us to create a vivid, enduring tapestry of the world that transcends the temporal nature of our individual lives. And increasingly, we use machines to preserve, analyze, and rationalize these traces.

At the same time, we have long attempted to bridge human and machine capabilities through structures that connect our incompatible interfaces. Think of Grand Central Station, a hub where we augment human locomotion with machine locomotion. We enable people to move faster and over greater distances by bridging two unique characteristics of humans and machines: fine-grained, autonomous, yet slow movement using our legs and grosser, prescribed, yet faster movement using engines and tracks.

What happens when we fuse these two worlds of human and machine capabilities? What happens when we capture the real world in a way that can be used by machines and *then* leverage that machine capacity to boost human capacities? That is the future of search, with its unique ability to index and make sense of the real world while at the same time acting as a universal interface to this knowledge. Search is the hinge we've always wanted.

Again, this is not search as we think of it today, an information retrieval system where we enter a noun and hope to get pages of results about that noun back. Instead, we must think of search as the omniscient watcher in the sky, aware of everything that is happening on the ground below. For this to happen, search itself needs to be deconstructed into its component tasks: indexing and understanding the world and everything in it; reading senses, so search systems can see and hear (and eventually smell and touch!) and interact with us in more natural ways; and communicating with us humans in contextually appropriate ways, whether that's in text, in speech, or simply by talking to other machines on our behalf to make things happen in the real world.

Over the next several chapters, we'll explore our progress in turning search into the hinge that links the unique abilities of humans and machines. We'll first examine this new web and the challenges search engines face. Next, we will look at what search engines will do given their new remit and we'll introduce the new rules for search engines. After we've gotten a solid grounding in the potential for what search will become, we will look at how this new generation of search will embrace a greater degree of humanity, augment our human abilities, and truly become our agent in the real and virtual worlds.

Despite the promising scenarios we in the tech field envision, the future of search is not assured. We will examine the obstacles that currently prevent us from ushering in the golden age of search, from the technical challenges to broader societal questions around whether we want this power of seemingly omnipresent insight about our world and everything in it. Finally, we will look at what search will mean when we hinge human potential with machine-level capabilities into a symbiotic relationship that radically upends existing notions of commerce, privacy, and the workings of our daily lives.

The Journey

So what picture of search will finally materialize? I have good news and bad news. The bad news is that no one *really* knows what's going to happen. That's also the good news. While there is no paucity of futurists who claim to see the logical, preordained outcome of this radical increase in the digital resolution of our analog world and the growth in the number of machines capable of understanding and acting on it, the stochastic and chaotic nature of both technology and societal mores lay the best predictions bare. So in this book, you are watching the picture take shape along with me. Even as I was writing, developments like Stephen Wolfram's Connected Devices Project and systems like IFTTT, which together allow devices to gain a measure of intelligence, popped up, about five years before I thought this capability would appear. That means my thinking was either startlingly obvious or startlingly prescient. In *Search*, we'll explore the emerging capacities of these new technologies by drawing on the ideas and research of some of the very best computer scientists, researchers, hardware developers, advertising execs, and good old-fashioned smart people. Together, we'll unpack this future, and hopefully what we find is a future that none of us would have predicted, but looking back it will appear as though there could have been no other.

So, at the end of this book will the location of the flying car be revealed? Will we finally see C3PO in the flesh rather than in CGI? While predicting technology tends to end in frustration, by the conclusion of this book, I hope we all agree that we are at a point in history where we have the pieces necessary to do more than just build logarithmic changes into our digital and physical lives. We are poised to make the leap from a society that views technology merely as a tool to do our bidding to a culture in which the symbiotic nature of machines and humans elevates us, our businesses, and our society to a higher plateau of existence and meaning.

CHAPTER 1

What Search Will See

There was a notion, when the Internet was first gaining consumer mindshare, that with it the infinite monkey theorem would be borne out much faster than had been previously thought. The theorem, developed by Èmile Borel, posited that a monkey randomly hitting keys on a typewriter would, over an infinite period of time, almost surely produce a work of Shakespeare. The capacity of the Internet was akin to multiplying the monkey by a million times; the underlying structure and massive scale of the web would enable *anything* to be created and described.

And, to an extent, that happened. The web was focused on text and images, and later, with YouTube, on video. By most accounts, the web in 1996 consisted of around 100,000 sites,[1] and if we use the standard metric of the time of around 441 pages per site, the size of the web was about forty-four million pages, or URLs. Today, modern indexers routinely see more than ten *trillion* URLs. Multiply that by the average number of words on a page, and you quickly start getting into numbers that boggle the human mind.

It's worth pausing here to talk about the evolution of the web for those of you who don't live in this world every second of every day. The web as we know it was conceived as a way to publish and link hypertext documents using a browser. Hypertext documents are nothing more than documents that have text that links to something else. Tim Berners-Lee, father of the World Wide Web, added a layer whereby those links pointed to another hypertext document stored elsewhere on a distributed network.

Over time, clever developers figured out how to make the web much more vibrant and active, but the underlying structure—along with the vast majority of content—was composed of documents linked to other documents. This is far from an indictment. In fact, such a structure was probably the only realistic thing that could have been done given the technology of the time. Remember that the world was a much slower, more analog-based place back in the late 1980s and early 1990s:

- Our computers were slower and incapable of displaying the complex graphics, videos, and photos that we see on even the cheapest devices today.
- Our connections were slower, so downloading anything other than characters took huge amounts of time. Those of you who remember 9600-baud modems will recall seeing words appearing across your screen as if they were produced by a very fast typist who was madly transcribing them from some remote location. As modems got faster, say 28.8 or 56k, we were able to see pictures and even hear some audio, but not without significant delays (and the dreaded slow-load of pictures on the web, which gradually resolved in as the data rushed down the wire).
- Our input methods were slower. With the exception of our computers, we didn't have digital anything. There were no digital cameras, no consumer digital recorders for audio, nothing. The only data that could be easily input and transmitted over computer networks were written documents.

• Our ability to capture more than text was limited. There was no GPS, no local database of places (hey kids, we used to get massive phone books dropped at our doorsteps once a year!), no sensors that figured out which direction you were pointed, and certainly no storage on our devices, even if we had been able to somehow manually digitize our surroundings. In 1989, a GB of space cost about $36,000 and was housed on forty heavy, magnetic hard drives. Today, 8GB costs less than $5 and can fit on your fingernail.

It's no wonder the web was built on top of text. There really was no other technical alternative.

A Brief History of Modern Search

Because the web was built with text documents, our initial attempt at cataloging it looked a lot like a primitive Dewey Decimal System. Yahoo was a hierarchical index curated by engineers; for a given word, there were sets of pages and websites that had relevance to that word. The hierarchical index was, and remains, effective as a signpost to broad destinations. If you are interested in Argentina hotels, a hierarchy can point you to a website that has lots of them.

As the web expanded from hundreds of thousands of pages to millions and then billions, and the words used on those pages expanded to the hundreds of trillions, a simple hierarchy no longer worked. And this is how search was born.

But there is a twist. An index on its own didn't make sense any more. An index is mainly used to find pages in *a single book* that correspond to a word or phrase. Certainly, an "index" that encompassed all the books in the library wouldn't be very useful; for a word like *elephants,* you'd have to wade through thousands of results across the hundreds of books housed in the library. And this realization started a revolution.

Search engineers realized that the books about elephants needed to be *ranked* in the index according to their relevance. Certainly, some books contained more relevant information about elephants (say, a book by an African author who lived with elephants for twenty years) than others (Disney's *Dumbo,* for example). Even in the non-digital world, creating such a ranked index was a challenge. How did you know whether the person lecturing you was actually an authority on horse breeding? How could you be sure the cave painting showed you the right way to spear bison? In the old days, authority was ranked, in many cases, by what others said about the sources—and that assessment was usually based on how often those sources gave people good information or helped them complete a task successfully. As search engines encompassed increasing amounts of human knowledge, engineers looked toward replicating that real-world paradigm inside our digital systems.

When Sergey Brin and Larry Page designed the BackRub algorithm that became Google, they weighted each of the results returned by a query. The weight corresponded to the perceived relevance of each result as it pertained to the query. They derived this weight by looking at the words on one page that were linked to another page on the web. These linked words (called *anchor text*) on page A provided search engines with descriptions of what the target page (page B) was likely about. When enough words of similar provenance pointed to a single page, say, if ten thousand pages all contained "elephant" anchor text that pointed to another, single page on the web (page B), engines would assume that page B was likely about elephants. Think of the process in relation to real life: if enough people tell you that the bathroom is on the second floor of the hotel, you will likely believe them. Your confidence in the answer is even greater if most of those people work in the hotel, because their authority on the topic is higher. The same is true of search: it isn't *just* that ten thousand pages tell engines that page B is about elephants; the quality of those ten thousand pages (their reputation) is an important evaluation factor.

There are hundreds of other variables that engineers developed over the years to help adapt search to the growing web. As the number of pages and links grew, our algorithms became better at discerning the meaning of the links and the other characteristics of web pages to help determine what users were likely looking for when they used a particular query.

In all cases, the search world was relatively simple, because we were searching for things in a relatively simple form. Words on pages—with the occasional picture—served as the fairly low-definition proxy for ideas in the real world.

The Trouble with Text

As the Internet grows, it begins to embody a more sophisticated representation of the world. It is no longer merely a set of pages and links with the occasional funny cat video, but a way for everything on the planet to be replicated, connected, and made useful. Given that goal, we are pushing against the limits of our traditional search systems. Namely, traditional search relies far too intensely on language as the primary way to interact with what is increasingly a digital copy of the physical world.

Language is a low-resolution way of describing the world.

The problem with language is that it's a "low-resolution" way of describing things. I'm sure there are those who will argue that nothing is more evocative than beautifully written prose that captures details as no picture ever could, and that it distills motivations, fears, and subtleties of human existence that aren't apparent on the surface. And they might be right. But try to define with language every attribute of a relatively simple object like a desk. The task would require tens of thousands of words: dimensions, materials, country of origin, the names of the people who assembled it, the refractory index of the finish, its location in the warehouse, the date of purchase. You'd create a tome just trying to capture all the elements that make up a simple desk in the physical world.

The rise of the digital circuit, ubiquitous networks, and practically unlimited storage changes our reliance on words as our way to describe everything around us, and offers us a way to describe the world and everything in it without us even having to do anything—the systems themselves, in many instances, catalog the world in which they exist. Welcome to a new reality: rather than having to write, draw, or paint to capture a moment, a feeling, or an object, we can now translate ten or one hundred times the amount of information about that moment with a device that fits in the palm of our hand, or can be attached to a car or stuck to a sliding glass door. Digital traces across the web left by machines and humans can be assembled to provide a more complete picture than we've ever had before of people, places, things, and events.

In other words, the search that we've grown up with worked because the best way we had to describe the world used a method that both search engines and we humans could comprehend: we understand words mapped to pages, and pages mapped to information and services. But wait, you might say, what about all the times I search for a video or image? The secret is this: until recently, even an image search just used text surrounding the image to find a match for what you were asking. Searching for "Batmobile" often returned results that had a caption or title of "Batmobile," even if the picture associated with it was of a bat riding in a toy car. The same goes for video search—unless appropriate keywords were somewhere on the YouTube page (or in the closed-captioned transcript), search wouldn't find it. In essence, when the only tool you have is a hammer, every problem looks like a nail.

But what happens when the virtual world is made up of much more than language-based descriptions of objects and ideas? What happens when the world is described in very fine detail not just by people, but by things? Soon, there will be fifteen billion connected devices—we're set to cross that threshold by 2015. These devices and sensors have a remarkable range of capabilities, from taking simple measurements like temperature, direction, and motion to performing more complex actions like transmitting images and videos. Suddenly, an Internet representation of a physical object like a bag of chips changes from a simple web page with nutritional content and some description to the following:

- Information about who "likes" the product
- Lists of local stores that carry it
- Opinions from people about the product and what they like/dislike about it
- Data on how often people buy the chips and the demographics of those buyers

This is a profound change that gets even more interesting when you apply it to all the other objects in the real world. No longer do we have to rely on language as a universal descriptor. Suddenly, the world can be modeled (a word we'll use often) in seemingly endless detail using facets that have little relation to language. Natural language and analog multimedia like books, photographs, records, and film are no longer the dominant descriptors of the world. The lingua franca of today's physical descriptions are aspects like location, time, associated people, abilities, and visual representations—these are the features that describe the material world, and increasingly these are digital descriptions stored on the web. Much like an electron microscope allows us to see the surface contours of a pollen spore, though we're only able to make out fuzzy details with the naked eye, the increasing digitization of the world means that everything is being described at a higher and higher resolution.

You can imagine, therefore, the plight of the poor search engines navigating today's web, trying to find words on pages when the "pages" often don't exist as such, and if they do, they often don't have "words." Imagine the engine trying to "find" your friend's recommendation for a restaurant in Vienna, which she mentioned to you two weeks ago during a meeting. It would be akin to a librarian walking into his library to find some books singing, while others changed their colors, some hid inside other books, others moved around on shelves to places they shouldn't be, and others couldn't be opened at all. Imagine how complex his job would be if he could only use his antiquated card catalog, indexed only with words and corresponding physical locations on stable shelving systems, to find anything. He would certainly switch careers. May I suggest computer science?

The More Capable Web

We are rapidly moving from an Internet composed chiefly of text pages to one I call the "capable web." While the majority of the web that we see still consists of content, hundreds of services—from Uber to TaskRabbit to Plated— have popped up in the last five years, transforming the web from an information repository to a vibrant tool that offers transport of data as well as a connecting bridge that allows things to happen in real life. Rather than existing as merely a

> The "capable web" lets people take action, not just find information.

digital version of the world's largest library, the capable web both stores information and enables people *to do things* in the real world.

In today's search, cracks begin to show quickly when you try to do things that expand past the noun-based search we've grown up with. For example, even though it is technically simple for a search engine to take a user directly to a reservation page for a given restaurant on OpenTable, today's engines don't do it. If I type in a phrase like "get a reservation tonight at 7pm at Wild Ginger," traditional search will, at best, return a set of pages from which I could take action. But that's not what I want—I want to complete my task without intermediary steps. I'd like the engine to know who I am, to know what I likely mean, and to find out if there is a table open tonight. If there's not, I'd like it to recommend a restaurant that I might like instead, based on my request and what it knows about me. But today's search gives us links to web pages because the engines still treat all queries as requests for documents, images, or video. But what happens when search stops treating the web as a big library and instead considers it a digital proxy for the physical world?

In order for search to evolve, it needs to make sense of and process the capable web, the makeup of which will evolve even in the months that pass between the time I write these words and the time you read them. To help us understand the milieu in which search can now work, let's take a moment to look at the tapestry of this global, capable web.

Images

Images have been part of the web since its earliest days, but the advent of camera phones and high-speed networks have increased exponentially the quantity and quality of images on the web. And it is not just that there are more of them; many of the images now have attributes attached that give them additional fidelity. From the latitude and longitude of the photo (which allows systems to understand where the photo was taken), the time it was taken, the name of the person who took it, the type of device used to take it, and tags of people in the photo, an image is now truly worth several thousand words. Combine that level of detail with the fact that we are now seeing *billions* of photos per day published to the web, and you get amazing resolution of the real world created daily. Further, as we'll learn later, systems are beginning to recognize what *is in the* photos, not simply catalog that they exist.

Video

While RealNetworks was the first to popularize web video, it wasn't until YouTube came along in 2006 that we went from expensive production and hosting of video content to something anyone could do on nearly any device. We have all heard the statistics—every minute there are twenty-five hours of video uploaded to YouTube. And just as with videos, the proliferation of devices like the Dropcam, Google Glass, and GoPro as well as increasingly sophisticated mobile phones will only accelerate this trend. Add facial recognition software to the characteristics we get with pictures, and suddenly we have high-fidelity descriptions of many situations on the planet. Systems like Koemei or Microsoft's MAVIS turn the audio track of videos into machine-readable text, making even videos searchable using today's systems.

Social Networks

Tomes have been written about new networks such as Twitter and Facebook; suffice it to say that the growth of these systems has been nothing short of explosive. As of mid-2013, people express their "likes" of people, places, things, and statuses on Facebook 4.5 billion times *per day*. They share more than 4 billion pieces of information *per day* on Facebook alone.

Anatomy of a "Like"

Let's take a moment and analyze the composition of a like: I attended an event in Dublin and posted a photo to my Facebook profile. I shared my location (The Long Room, Trinity College, for which Facebook has an entire page), who I am with (Sarah Elizabeth Ippel, my partner, which Facebook also tells you), and the time that I'm there.

Also important is who "likes" the post. One challenge: at present, we're not sure what people are liking. Is it coworkers liking that I'm out of the country? Do people like the picture? Or do they like the fact that I referenced a Harry Potter location? All we know at this point is that two of my friends, Naveen and Ayelet, both "like" something about it—but who can guess what? For a search system, it's trivial to then examine each of those people's profiles to understand what they *likely* like about the post. Does Ayelet often post about Harry Potter? Is Naveen frequently in Dublin? The ability for a system to figure out what people "like" in the photo is thus extended, thanks to the preferences they show when they are online and connected.

We also see comments, including one from my friend Curt, who mentioned he was just there, a fact that the overall system can use to build a good profile of Curt. This illustration is not meant to cause alarm; after all, I opted in to all of this and could easily restrict privacy and settings to very cloistered levels. The point is that, with a ten-second update from my phone, I have contributed dozens of signals that can be used to elaborate the physical world in digital form.

Personal Information

Facebook and LinkedIn are two of the most prevalent sources of personal data today. And the data is not confined to what people share explicitly in their profiles—it includes what they share implicitly on their merry way across the web. Think about your Internet use and consider how many sites actually use Facebook or LinkedIn as a route to log in. But it's more than just login: these services also get limited personal data from Facebook or LinkedIn. So the next thing I know, TaskRabbit has my home address or a conference website has my title, the length of time I've been in my position, and a head shot.

It isn't just about Facebook having the data, it's about all the sites in the world that use that identity that now have it. This spread of your "self" is a profound change in the Internet ecosystem, and one that wasn't really possible until the rise of Facebook and its federated login system. In the future, we'll likely have a single authentication system for the web, whether it's via Facebook, Microsoft, Google, or any other service; all the other services we use can accrete their specific domain-level information back to that central ID store. So when you use SpotHero to reserve space in a parking garage, for example, that information can flow back to your central ID, making every other application or service that uses the ID more powerful and personal.

Services

One of the high-potential new entrants into the more capable web is what I call "connected reality." We have read for years in science fiction about systems that can *do* things for us in the real world. Things happening on our behalf out in the world, without us consciously having to do them, is the stuff of nerd magic—whether we're looking at a dystopian future like the one in *The Terminator*, which features a cloud-connected autonomous killing machine, or are considering something more delightful, like personal medallions that serve as beacons to open doors, turn on lights, or play messages from people who have stopped by the house. In the past five years we have seen an explosion of services that connect virtual events to physical applications. Following are just a few examples:

• SpotHero and QuickPay find you parking in a garage or on a street, let you pay for it virtually, and ensure that the spot is available when you get there. In addition, they manage real-time inventory of parking spaces and publish that data to the web for consumption by other services.

• INRIX and Waze use the powerful supercomputers (also known as smartphones!) in our pocket to measure our speed and position and report that information back to a central service. The result? You can be routed to your destination in the most optimal manner. Even if the freeway is shorter by distance, it might not be the best course; these systems plot your route over roads less traveled to save you time and frustration.

• OpenTable pioneered the digital-to-physical transition in the early 2000s and is still going strong, connecting unreserved restaurant seats with people who wish to occupy them.

• Postmates, a one-hour delivery service, and TaskRabbit, a resource for accomplishing household errands and skilled tasks, turn a desire (for example, "I want a phone charger in the next hour" or "I need someone to scrape my ceiling and take the paint chip to an asbestos testing lab") into an action.

• IFTTT (If This, Then That) combines a number of online services then brokers the actions when something happens in one of them. If I take a picture with my phone, IFTTT will post it automatically to my Facebook page, save it to my OneDrive, and tweet my followers that I've captured another amazing piece of digital flotsam. Anything is possible with this system, including such fun directives as, "Unlock my chocolate box when I hit ten thousand steps in a day as measured by my Fitbit."

• SmartThings connects the real and virtual worlds, using cheap door/window, motion, and temperature sensors to take action; if a sensor detects moisture near my water heater, for example, the system will text me an alert. Or when there is no motion in my condo for thirty minutes, the system shuts off all the lights.

• GateGuru stitches together hundreds of data points to tie together your flight itineraries, airport security wait times, and curated lists of airport food, shops, and services, including more than twenty-five thousand reviews and tips and five thousand photos of airports, terminals, and airport amenities.

• SeatGeek applies data to the real world by tracking the special events happening in your chosen locations and associating the two hundred-plus ticket brokers to those events, so you don't overpay for that Taylor Swift concert.

• Uber connects you with taxis, drivers for hire, and ride-sharing services in real time and is now moving into same-day deliveries.

• Seamless satisfies your need for Chinese food on a Tuesday in your loft by connecting you to local restaurants that deliver.

- Dozens of retail services and apps save you a trip to the store by finding the product you want in stock and letting you reserve it for pickup.

In every case, these new services create "hooks" that enable people to accomplish something quickly and conveniently, with just a few taps on their smartphone or tablet screens. Albert Einstein described quantum physics as "spooky action at a distance"—the same is happening right before our eyes without the need for string theory!

Devices

Thousands of words have been written about the magic of the shrinking microprocessor and the number of sensors we carry around in our pockets. Until a couple of years ago, these sensors were primarily limited to our smartphones, but with GPS, accelerometers, gyroscopes, clocks, and compasses, together with Wi-Fi triangulation and signaling, near field communication, and Bluetooth communication, we now have the ability to measure hundreds of aspects of our existence and feed the information back to one or more services. But we're getting even beyond these types of measurements:

- Devices like Google Glass, with its ability to capture constant imagery of what you are seeing, or the Microsoft LifeCam which captures shots every few seconds, mean that people can create a continual, permanent digital record of their lives.

- Autographer, a wearable, hands-free camera available today, has five separate sensors that record your life in real time, including temperature, photos, global positioning, compass direction, and rate of motion. Now you never have to take a picture again when you're on vacation, as everything is recorded for you.

• Real-time transcription, heralded by innovations like Intel's new Edison chip, means that every conversation you have could be captured and transcribed for later retrieval—and those conversations are now tagged with a location, time, and potentially even the name of the person to whom you are speaking, if the person is on your calendar. Or if the person is captured with your Google Glass or checks in to the same physical location that you do within a few minutes of your check-in. You get the idea.

"Things"

As we discussed earlier, plunging hardware costs have a dramatic effect on the cacophony of the Internet. The rise of tools to design and manufacture single- or few-purpose devices that can measure, analyze, report, and even affect their environment has led to the "Internet of Things," whereby the web can extend its reach beyond the virtual and into our collective offline existence.

• Low-power and inexpensive chips mean that devices like magnetometers epoxied to the street in Los Angeles can run for years without needing a new battery. These devices can tell when a car is parked in a spot. And of course, that is more geolocated data fed to the cloud: a parking space located at XX latitude and YY longitude is empty or full at this precise time. Every second of every day.

• Personal tracking devices indicate where I am, how fast I am moving, how many steps I have taken and when I have taken them, my galvanic response, my heart rate, my pupil dilation when viewing an image, and more. Devices that track some of these functions are already in existence, and the others will be added in the near future. Imagine your glasses recording that your heart rate increases and your pupils dilate when you look at something you find interesting. The notion of explicitly "liking" something will seem like writing a letter to an editor.

• Gadgets that have been quietly activating a switch in response to a stimulus—like the Clapper or a motion sensor on your garage—suddenly get the gift of communication. Rather than just turning on a light when you clap your hands, for example, they can now talk to other devices in your home, or anywhere in the world, to coordinate their actions.

• The lock on your door becomes more than a mechanism for keeping people out—it becomes an input for a system to learn who is likely to be home and when.

Events

The flyers tacked up in the dorm bathroom or on the bulletin board at work advertising upcoming events have morphed into a number of online services that enable searching and sharing of events across the world. Moreover, the digitization of these notices means they can be accessed from anywhere.

With the advent of cheap online conferencing, people don't even have to be in the same physical location to participate in something they care about. Companies like Meetup and Eventbrite, along with networks like Facebook, make organizing simple and inherently viral. Other companies, like the Twitter-acquired Spindle, mined the mass of data being added to the cloud to capture what was really happening in a city, in addition to the official sources. Imagine being able to listen to every conversation across a metro area and divining what was happening based on that—that is what Spindle did using text, audio, pictures, and video.

Places

While completely virtual events are gaining in popularity, most events are still rooted in physical locations. There are dozens of systems today that capture the intricate details of physical spaces, from theater websites that show their seat map and capacity to Yelp's descriptions of bars and restaurants. Moreover, we now have ways to understand in real time what is happening at each location, whether it's via check-ins on Foursquare or a recent Microsoft patent that uses microphones on cell phones to report the noise level of a venue to the cloud, to understand whether the location is busy or empty. The data gathered by resident sensors can inform a multitude of decisions.

And consider this: more than twenty-five million small businesses have active company pages on Facebook, allowing them to communicate with their customers and prospective customers in near real time. These pages feature special offers, the company's hours of operation, people who like the brand or product, and events. Essential information about the business that would once have been described in real life has now migrated online to augment the concept of "place."

Hybrid Systems

There are a number of systems that allow for digitization of the real world in ways that add a higher layer of fidelity to temporal events. While the following services may not seem revolutionary, consider them among many thousands of data sources to which people are contributing aspects of their world. When those captures are stitched together, they represent people, places, and experiences in all their glorious detail—and that's truly spectacular.

• Services like FanFootage out of Dublin allow people to use their smartphones to record live events such as concerts; FanFootage's proprietary system then stitches all those pieces of footage together into a coherent whole. Imagine being able to watch the concert from a thousand different angles—even more impressive, in many cases they are able to use the soundboard recording from the concert as audio, turning grainy, poor audio recordings into beautiful concert footage with crisp music.

• Foodspotting is a service that allows people to share pictures of their restaurant meals (which, of course, can be cross-referenced with the restaurant's site); the dishes are all shareable and searchable, so you can find what you're craving or see what's good either at a given restaurant or in your area.

Payment Systems

We've had widespread consumer digital payment services since PayPal launched in 1999, but most were restricted to online purchases. You could use PayPal to send friends money for a dinner at which you split the check, but the majority of transactions were related to e-commerce. But PayPal has evolved—as have Square and VeriFone—to allow small businesses and sole proprietors to handle digital payments easily and quickly. Sending money is now as easy as sending an e-mail, and the rise of new currencies like Bitcoin show how value can be exchanged even without a backing central currency. In short, it's increasingly possible for systems to broker transactions both with and without human intervention. And the ability for all these transactions to be known by search is growing—so a system will know that I don't shop at Barneys but often purchase from Bluefly, and it will be smart enough to know that I like nice clothes but never pay retail.

Big Data, Bigger Implications

Physical objects, places, people, and interactions are all being digitized, and that information can be utilized in some form or fashion by other systems. This aggressive digitization represents a sea change—it is the biggest and most rapid advance of information and modeling in human history.

For example, in the old world, one of the biggest advances in public parking was a system of lights across the ceiling of a parking garage that showed, at a glance, where the open spots were located. This was a great, albeit gross, way to reduce the problem of finding a parking place down to a point where one could save significant amounts of time. Rather than driving down each aisle, a driver could spot a green light across the garage and skip the aisles topped by a line of red lights. The scope of the solution—much like the cave drawings or an index of a book—was local. A driver had to enter the garage without knowing whether there were any open spots inside or where they were.

Just two years later there are sensors directly in the street (or parking garage)—these self-powered, relatively cheap magnetometers can detect the metal in a car and thus determine whether there is a car in a particular spot. The sensors communicate the status of each and every spot via low-power Wi-Fi to repeaters on light poles and then to a central cloud service. Suddenly, there's an entirely new scenario: before they even start looking for spots, drivers are directed to just the right place at the right time. But even more importantly, engines on the web are now able to consume this real-time information and use it in a way that benefits drivers and businesses (the parking garage, in this case).

And this machine-level intelligence is not just being deployed in large, public places. The capacity for average people to benefit from this mass digitization in their homes and everyday lives is upon us. Let me paint you a picture of the ten minutes that transpired when I arrived home this evening.

- During my drive home, hundreds of discrete measurements about my direction, speed, and driving habits were captured by an app on my phone and fed to a cloud service that paints real-time pictures of traffic conditions.
- As I enter my condo, a $30 wireless sensor implanted on my door registers my arrival and communicates with another cloud service to ask what should happen at this time of the day when that door opens. The cloud service, in turn, talks to a number of light switches in my condo and tells them that, since it's after sundown, a number of them should turn on.
- I ask my Xbox to power on and, as it has performed facial and skeletal recognition using its Kinect camera, it loads my profile, catalog, and preferences from across all the devices I use (my phone, my work computer, and my tablet). Because I left my office in the middle of watching a TED Talk (and my office tablet dutifully informed the video cloud service of that fact), the Xbox offers that as a place from which to start.
- Meanwhile, my phone registers that it has entered an approximate physical location that corresponds to my condo address. As I had set a location reminder earlier in the day, my phone prompts me to pick up a package from the front desk that was delivered while I was at the office.

It is also logs the time I arrived at home and stores that information for later analysis.

- I notice an alert on the tablet I left on my coffee table—it says my fridge got too hot today, and, sure enough, I didn't shut the door all the way before I left.
- My small window camera has been capturing the myriad designs of the Ferris wheel on the Seattle Waterfront all day.
- My smart plugs have been quietly recording my condo's energy usage and turning off devices that don't need power.
- And my thermostat recorded motion in the house, taking note and building a model for my routine on this particular day of the week.

There are people who have many more sensors in their homes, cars, appliances, and devices than I do, and obviously there are those with far fewer. But this level of instrumentation will not be an outlier in five years. If you look at coverage of 2014's Consumer Electronics Show, you will see the dozens of companies and hundreds of products emerging that offer low-cost sensors, wireless connectivity, and either proprietary or open services to take advantage of the "chatter" of devices.

A Capable Web Fueled by Devices

Part of the growth in connectivity is arising from the lower capital investment required to build "chatty" devices. The cost to produce, distribute, and replace both the hardware and the software necessary to create these little capturers of reality has fallen by several orders of magnitude. In fact, the only cost associated with the production of these sensors that has likely increased is the cost of the education required to learn how to build them. And even that cost is under pressure from a combination of factors like MOOCs (Massive Open Online Courses) and design and programming tools that are increasingly more like word processors than traditional development environments.

Jeremy Conrad, cofounder of hardware incubator Lemnos Labs in San Francisco, thinks a lot about how the companies he brings into his lab can ride this cost curve to create the next-generation web. The incubator has birthed some products that would have been simply impossible even a decade ago. As a case in point: a company called Nanosatisfi, for just over a million dollars, built a satellite that lets anyone take photos and conduct science experiments in space. Let that sink in—for little more than a million dollars a company designed and launched space satellites that we mortals can access. They even managed to tap into the sharing economy, buying space capacity on rockets that were already going up, because Nanosatisfi's satellites weigh so little. Contrast that with some satellite averages—a normal imaging satellite weights 4 tons, costs $850 million dollars, and takes up an entire cowling of a rocket.

Beyond incredible examples like Nanosatisfi's satellite, there are other hardware and software systems that are becoming more accessible to more users. For example, Conrad tells us:

In the early 1980s when CAD [computer-aided design] systems first came out they were at $100,000 in 1980 dollars. They actually came with a desk and a computer because there was no assumption that you would have a computer to load the software on. If you fast-forward to 2003 when I had my first internship in aerospace, computers that could run the software were still like $10,000 or $15,000 and then the software was still $10,000 to $15,000. So you were looking at maybe

> Hardware design costs have fallen by three orders of magnitude in thirty-five years.

$20,000 to $30,000 for a really amazing work station. Then, if you fast-forward to today, my companies can buy a $400 desktop and there are free CAD packages. If you just look at that one thing, you've seen a drop of three orders of magnitude in thirty-five years.

Part of the radical change in pricing is the advent of manufacturing systems that allow designers to rapidly prototype and fail without expensive "tooling costs." Traditionally, tens of thousands of dollars had to be spent to make a mold for the plastic case of a device—and that investment had to be made before the first device was produced or the first customer sale took place. Today, with the reduction in pricing and a huge increase in the availability of medium-quality 3D printers, an entrepreneur or company can have an idea for a product and go through dozens of prototypes for the cost of some plastic. Inventors don't even have to buy the machines; small companies like Protomold can take your 3D design file and produce a small run of your part or component for less than $2,000. Small injection mold runs like this were at one time possible only if you could commit to buying a huge run at a later time. Such obstacles obviously hamper the innovation ability of small dreamers and curtail the spread of these devices, but advances in technology are making development processes accessible to more people.

Finally, there is new appetite for the funding side of hardware. Ten years ago, a company needed to raise $10 to 15 million just to get a piece of hardware out the door. An entrepreneur or company didn't design a device without an entire business plan in place, including distribution through big-box retailers, which meant they had to be ready to go from idea to Best Buy immediately. Venture capitalists, with their need for a double-digit internal rate of return and a 10x return on their investments, would obviously be loathe to invest in a ton of manufacturing. Today, many of the pieces are trivial in cost, making initial funding rounds smaller, with more of them spurring innovation through more players in the space. And then there are the customers. It was once hard to find customers and relatively difficult to interact with them directly, but the connection points offered by the Internet have led to a profound shift; instead of being merely "customers," today's consumers are more akin to "partners." As Conrad said:

> Before, if you wanted to sell a new device, you could sell in big-box stores. But pre-big-box stores, what were your options? There were local stores, but now you're talking specialty stores with long sales cycles or you could buy catalogue placement in the back of *Popular Science,* which was very popular for the longest time. Now we have things like crowdfunding or buying advertising on a search engine—you can actually get access to those first few thousand early adopter customers all over the United States in hours, days, or, at most, a couple of weeks.

Crowdfunding sites like Kickstarter allow all of us to be mini investors in the hardware revolution, spurring the number of connected devices in a way most of us would not have thought possible a decade ago. For well under $1,000, I have purchased online Internet-connected watches, a home automation system, a voice-controlled assistant, and innovative cables and chargers—before I even touched any of them. And none of these products would have been possible, either technically or physically, using the production methods available a few years ago.

So what about scale once an investment or idea pays off?

How do we go from a few thousand units to millions if the innovator gets it right? While much ink has been spilled on the rise of Chinese manufacturing, the real news is that the price of shipping parts from China to your markets is a practically infinitesimal portion of the cost. Of course there is a cost, but thanks to the humble cargo container (brilliantly explained in Marc Levinson's book *The Box*), moving your product from the manufacturing site to the customer costs you time but far less treasure than it once did.

This is all to say that the ability for an entrepreneur to dream up something in her bedroom, model it on a cheap PC and free CAD/CAM program, prototype both plastics and circuits in a shared lab, and sell the first thousand units without ever leaving her house has yielded—and will yield an even greater—explosion of devices that can contribute data about the real world to the ever-increasing appetite of our search engines.

A Capable Web Fueled by Ubiquitous Communication

Former editor of *Wired* magazine and best-selling author Chris Anderson famously talked about the peace dividend of the smartphone war. He pointed out that the prices of smartphones have shrunk dramatically because the components—all the elements from GPS to radios to screens to memory to processors—are being produced in vast quantities for the hundreds of millions of smartphones sold each year. That means other electronics that use these components benefit from massive economies of scale and thus also become markedly cheaper, more disposable, and ubiquitous.

But I contend that the smartphone peace dividend actually means something else. It's not just that companies can now use mass-produced cell phone components to build other things—like a tiny, inexpensive camera that records your entire day, and sells for $229 (plus a $9 per month subscription), as does the Narrative product—it's that smartphones increasingly are the hub of your connected life. The reason so many devices can add information about the world to the web is that they use your smartphone as the gateway. My smartwatch from Martian would cost much more, last a fraction as long, and be far bulkier if it had to include radios that could talk to cell towers. Instead, because it uses my phone as a bridge to the web, all it needs is a simple, cheap, low-power Bluetooth radio.

The number of devices, especially portable devices, is naturally constrained by their primary connection method to the web. For example, I generally can't have more than one Bluetooth device talking to my phone at the same time. Tethering via Wi-Fi still isn't as easy as it should be on devices without screens. But even this is likely a temporary problem. Radio frequency is a finite resource—you can't make any more radio waves. That said, much of the spectrum is underutilized. The vast majority of Americans who have switched to digital television no longer use the analog signals that once delivered our network television. Without going into the physics involved, freeing up this lower-frequency spectrum means that devices can use lower power (and therefore less battery) and still communicate across vast ranges. The screen and radio are the two biggest power consumers in a wireless device, so as we get better and more efficient radio technology, devices will no longer need to rely on a cell phone to gain access to the larger connected intelligence of the web.

Other radio innovations are coming, too. Picocells (small base stations that use the same frequencies our devices do) have proven very effective at increasing network capacity

Soon, devices won't need your cell phone in order to talk to the web.

in dense-usage areas. Used on a large scale, picocells could greatly reduce the power draw on small devices, as the radios inside our devices could talk to a "tower" closer to their location.

There are also bridging techniques. A few years ago I worked on a project that turned a PC into a transceiver, allowing others to use that PC's Internet connection to surf the net. Much like people tether their computer to their phone, this solution allowed a host PC to use newly vacated "white space" airwaves (today residing at around 700 MHz) while the other devices used a low-power radio on a different frequency to talk to the host.

The team at Commotion, which uses mobile phones, computers, and other wireless devices to create decentralized mesh networks, is working on bringing a similar product to market. Additional trials are testing whether devices can be made smart enough to share the federal spectrum beyond 700 MHz when government agencies aren't using it, while giving the agencies priority when they need it. Other organizations, like the Serval Project, are exploring frequencies like those used by cordless phones to create mini-networks that can link devices, even without any infrastructure in place. Ultimately, these concepts rely on devices working together to balance the load of web requests, voice calls, and funny cat videos across the available spectrum each device can access at the optimal power load.

No matter how we bridge the gap between devices and their ability to communicate on their own (and we will), it will enable another order of magnitude of smart little devices that will monitor, chatter, and ultimately give us unprecedented insight into our world.

Understanding the Physical World with the Capable Web

As we've discussed, the structure of search was built around the world as it existed at the time. The search we all know centered around the web of words; now it's time to shift our thinking to the web of the world. As we do, we see search systems now have the raw data to start making sense of the world. Indeed, just last year researchers at Google were surprised when their machine learning systems discovered how to identify faces without explicitly being told how. In other words, the systems were able—in much the same way we are—to build mental models to answer the question, "What is a face?"

Traditional models required computer scientists to program *features* into a system to help it classify items it comes across. Very simply, a feature is a measurable characteristic of an object. A feature of an apple might be the RGB values for its color or the length of its stem. In search, we often combine a number of features to broadly classify things we find. It's like saying to a system, "If you see an oval object with these dimensions, a couple of indentations spread more or less equally apart with a protuberance in the middle, and an opening approximately two-thirds down the oval below the protuberance, that is likely a face" (although the language we use is not English, but rather mathematical algorithms). While this is certainly an effective model, there is an inherent scale problem—think of the trillions of objects we might want to classify. A programmer or information scientist must consciously think about everything in the world and how to describe the features of all those things, and then he must program the model—usually with computer code—so the system can recognize objects it finds.

Contrast that with human learning, which happens naturally

through pattern recognition. No one tells a baby that down is down, up is up, hard things hurt, and soft things cushion. We learn these things without being told, through observation, by trial and error, and by developing patterns in our minds of familiar objects like a "face" or a "pillow." But there are limits.

For humans, a phenomenon called *inattentional blindness* trains our overloaded brains to ignore things that aren't directly relevant to the task at hand. Give me ten thousand pictures, ask me to find the ones where a cylindrical trash can appears in the background, and tell me I can spend only a limited amount of time on the task, and I will likely miss most of them. Machines don't suffer from inattentional blindness—with a machine, every pixel can be analyzed, every piece of data can be reconciled, every bit can be cross-referenced. Timescales can be compressed by spreading the task across thousands or millions of processors. They are relentless, indefatigable, and stoic.

Even so, it was a little surprising when, late in 2013, systems began to beat humans at identifying objects in a picture *when the machine hadn't been trained to do so*. In this case, the object was a paper shredder sitting in the background of an image. The challenge, as alluded to above, is how a developer would describe to a computer in

In 2013, a machine taught itself to recognize real-world objects.

any level of detail what a paper shredder looks like. And even if a good description could be constructed for a straight-on view, the moment the object is turned at a forty-five-degree angle, problems mount.

Indeed, the system figured the task out on its own, though the programmer did give the machine the goal of finding objects in the pictures. But, even though the scientist couldn't comprehensively describe a paper shredder, the system eventually divined what a shredder looked like. And the system was able to complete the task more quickly and accurately than its human counterparts. According to an article in the *Register* late last year, "This means that for some things, Google researchers can no longer explain exactly how the system has learned to spot certain objects, because the programming appears to think independently from its creators, and its complex cognitive processes are inscrutable. This 'thinking' is within an extremely narrow remit, but it is demonstrably effective and independently verifiable."[2]

"Great," you're saying, "machines can now figure out what a paper shredder looks like in a room. This is progress?" It is—but it's only half the magic. Or maybe you are saying, "Whoa, did you just say computers are thinking? Didn't we see a movie about this starring the former governor of California that did not end well?" The fact that a computer can learn to identify a paper shredder isn't in itself going to revolutionize search. But when systems are able to join individual islands of discovery together, the ability for our systems to not just see but understand the world in which they exist means that they will be cognizant participants in our shared reality rather than rote retrievers of data.

Stitching Together Reality

Humans don't see or think about things in isolation. We see one object in our world, and that sight perhaps triggers a thought about the last place we saw the object, which then causes us to think about who we were with, and that causes us to think about how that person is doing, the company she started, and the industry it was in. Finally, we might think about some news we read the day before that related to the industry in which our friend's company operates, and we think we might want to call her and let her know. All of these thoughts cascade from a simple object sitting on a counter. In

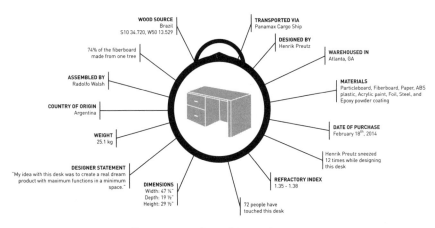

WOOD SOURCE
Brazil
S10 34.720, W50 13.529

TRANSPORTED VIA
Panamax Cargo Ship

DESIGNED BY
Henrik Preutz

74% of the fiberboard
made from one tree

WAREHOUSED IN
Atlanta, GA

ASSEMBLED BY
Radolfo Walsh

MATERIALS
Particleboard, Fiberboard, Paper, ABS
plastic, Acrylic paint, Foil, Steel, and
Epoxy powder coating

COUNTRY OF ORIGIN
Argentina

DATE OF PURCHASE
February 18th, 2014

WEIGHT
25.1 kg

Henrik Preutz sneezed
12 times while designing
this desk

DESIGNER STATEMENT
"My idea with this desk was to create a real dream
product with maximum functions in a minimum
space."

DIMENSIONS
Width: 47 ¼"
Depth: 19 ½"
Height: 29 ½"

REFRACTORY INDEX
1.35 - 1.38

72 people have
touched this desk

FIGURE 1-1: An illustration of an object's features

the same way, search systems that understand the real world in all its gory detail will derive associations and understandings from objects. When search finally understands every characteristic (or feature) of every object on the planet, it will be able to make connections that, due to its sheer speed and scale, won't even be visible to us humans.

Imagine that we have sets of amazingly described objects within a search system. Not just a few, but millions of sets. As of spring 2014, Bing has 33 billion object descriptions inside its knowledge repository: it has descriptions for almost 2 million wine bottles; 800,000 movies; 1.2 billion people. But where this gets interesting is that these different sets of data (wine bottles and restaurants that serve bottles of wine, for example) share commonalities, and this is where the power begins to become more obvious; rather than simply understanding an object, systems can use that knowledge to understand exponential numbers of *other* objects.

In math and computer science, we call these connections between things *graphs*. Graphs are simply a way to represent how things relate to one another. So a *social graph* for Stefan shows who he knows, where he lives (relating a place to Stefan), what he likes (relating real-world objects or events to

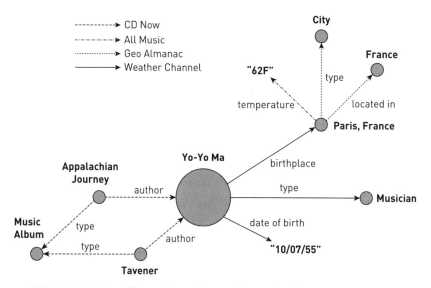

FIGURE 1-2: An illustration of a set of "graphs"[3]

Stefan), and so on. The challenge is in linking discrete graphs: the social graph (think of the information contained in Facebook and LinkedIn), the geospatial graph (think of maps and local data from Zagat, Frommer's, Yelp, TripAdvisor, etc.), the action graph (think of all the apps in app stores and the actions they help people perform in the real world), the event graph (consider Meetup, Evite, Craigslist, Ticketmaster, etc.), and hundreds more.

The mission is to find the commonalities among these graphs so we can begin to assemble a complete picture of the world and everything in it. We'll talk more about this later, but the ability we now have to see any single thing from many different angles across many graphs represents a profound leap. Remember the past, when the world could be described only in words and moving or still pictures? Every person and object is now being described in hundreds of ways—from your crowdsourced

> Graphs allow us to understand every object from a nearly infinite set of angles.

photos on Flickr to your weight as reported by your connected scale to the energy consumed by the printer plugged into your smart outlet. We are entering a world where everything will be able to express itself in some way, either latently or explicitly. Once that happens, it's up to the machines to build models that begin to re-create reality, becoming more aware and more capable of being our smart assistant rather than our slave.

Let's think about our paper shredder again. The system knows the object is a shredder, and that one of its features is the opening size on the top. At the same time, the system has modeled a cat and hundreds of its features. How has it done this? The notion of a "cat" has been described across millions of pages on the web. Whether it's poetry written as an homage to a cat, a collection of cute videos, a medical journal on kitty cancer, an American Cat Fanciers Association breeding page, or one of tens of millions of others, the concept of a cat is pretty well modeled in thousands of forms. The systems employed by the major search engines these days are doing what they can to reassemble all these pieces of cat description into a coherent whole. Metaphorically, the *cat* in the real world has exploded and little pieces of him have been scattered across the web; it has been "decohered." It's now the job of these smarter machines to collect all these pieces of information from trillions of locations on the web and stitch together a picture of our feline friend.

Now that search systems have built this understanding of what a cat is, imagine the power of linking information across the graphs. The system understands the opening of the shredder from our information store where the shredder is described. The system also understands the general physical size of a cat, based on its coherence mission. The system, because of the linked graphs, knows the cat is too big to fit into the top of the shredder, should it ever be asked to do that.

You may protest this very odd example and say, "You shouldn't put a cat into a shredder because you will kill it—how do you teach a machine that killing is incompatible with established mores?" The good news is that the same types of calculations that let the system know a cat will not fit into the shredder's opening can apply, building a sense of morality into our systems as they become acquainted with all the information available across graphs. When the system figures out that a shredder does its work using sharp blades, that blades cut flesh, that cut flesh bleeds, and that exsanguination tends to stop something from being alive, and cats are usually alive, the system would likely come to the same conclusion even if it *could* fit the cat in the shredder. It will know it shouldn't put the cat in the shredder because that action would be incompatible with the normal state of a cat (i.e., that it is alive).[4]

But beyond preserving cats, this cornucopia of information on the web has benefits. As in the example above, graphs can be linked so the systems can make sense of the physical world in which they reside. They can learn language (a *jaguar* is both a car and an animal). They can understand relationships and causation (an oven is hot, chicken is dangerous when raw due to bacteria, bacteria can't survive above a certain temperature, an oven can heat chicken to that temperature), and actions as they relate to the things the system has modeled (you can *buy* tickets to a *movie*, you can *eat sushi* at *Shiro's*, you can *read* a *book* on a *Kindle*).

Indeed, there will be skeptics. They will point out that the above chicken example is nothing more than a logical syllogism that can be wrong as often as it is right. After all another way to kill bacteria would be to use bleach. And while using bleach on chicken would accomplish the first objective (killing harmful bacteria), without other conditions in place to prevent that action (conditions such as: humans can't consume chlorine above certain concentrations without becoming sick, and a sick human is worse than a well human), the result would be disastrous.

This explosion of data is both an opportunity and a challenge. There has never been as much data available about the real world as exists now. But data itself is not the answer; we are drowning in data. In order to achieve a quantum leap in search and achieve levels of omniscience only dreamt of, we must rethink the problems search can be used to solve. Rather than performing simple retrieval tasks, search should grow to be our "hinge," facilitating a collaboration between the human and the digital. Search should be a partner, a teacher, a curator. It should appear when you need it as collaborator, but it should also nudge you transparently to make better decisions and push you toward actions that yield better outcomes.

Search should inspire our imagination, not deny us exercise of it. It should be generative, triggering an ever increasing cavalcade of thoughts and helping our own minds push our limits rather than restrict them.

Search is about what *can* be or what might be—allowing for chance, serendipity, and the occasional error—not what *is*. As we will see in the following chapters, search will enhance our own humanity in ways that equalize us, giving power to those without and helping to erase inherent bias and disability. Search has the potential to be the most transformative and enduring gift of the modern age.

So what does that world look like?

CHAPTER 2

How Search Will Act

When search has better optics about the world, it will have the key piece it needs to become more helpful in our everyday lives. As we saw in the previous chapter, search is gaining insights into information and processes that were previously locked inside proprietary systems—either our human brains (in the cases of relationships, attitudes, desires, and more) or within corporate and academic fiefdoms. These traces of humanity and society—often tiny in isolation but powerful when cohered—point to new capabilities for search that seem less like the model we've grown up with over the past seventeen years and more like the *Star Trek* computer dangled in front of us in the 1960s.

In this chapter, we will examine what this new "capable web" means for search, what needs to happen in order for search to process the new web, and how that ultimately sets search up to give powers to us. But first, we need some grounding on the state of the state.

So far we've talked about the historical role of search and how the structure of the early web dictated its development. We have also seen how search has been bound by the information available to the system. Finally, we've seen that the new, more capable web is made up of more than just text and images: it is flooded with trillions of pieces of data and service that systems can use to *do things*, not just *find information*.

What does all this mean for the future of search—not just for users, but also for producers, enterprises, and, ultimately, society? It means, for one, that we have to change our expectations for what search is and what it can do for us—we must demand more.

Search today is centered around what is called *known-item search* in information science parlance. With known-item search, you know that the item you are searching for exists and you only have to give an engine some hints to retrieve it. But what happens when you don't know what you are searching for? What if you aren't "searching" at all?

It's easy to become overwhelmed when you think about the predicament. How would you go about querying something like, "What is the best Bluetooth headset for me?" Today, you would likely go to a search engine, issue a query term like "best Bluetooth headsets," and then page through tens of links, clicking on each and reading the articles. You would need to decide how authoritative or authentic each article or page was, and you would have to sift through hundreds of words of irrelevant content, *especially* if all you cared about was size and battery life. There is no such thing as a "best" Bluetooth headset for a search engine to find; there is no "known item." Using a search engine to handle fuzzy queries rather than definitive ones like, "What is the population of Zambia?" often causes the searcher to perform many of the steps to find the solution he is looking for.

And that is where the next generation of search, using the more capable web, comes in. As we've said, search will be the hinge that brings together what systems are good at and what humans are intrinsically able to do. But before we move into what search will do, I'd like to outline some principles by which this next generation of search experiences will abide.

- Search will consist of a number of functions that work together in response to a query.

- A search "query" won't be words, necessarily; it will include any change in state. The change could be filling a blank search box with keywords or the change could be you waking up in Macau rather than in your home in Iowa.
- Search won't need to listen to what you say to know what you mean.
- Search will understand and take action in the real world rather than just observing it.
- Search will appear when and where you need it, even if you don't know you need it.
- Search will contribute to human knowledge, not simply index it.
- Search will simplify our lives, performing tasks we don't want to do, helping us make quality decisions, and ultimately steering us away from actions that are not to our benefit.

One Size Doesn't Fit All

So what *should* search do? I'd like to recommend that we stop thinking about that question as one with a single answer. Search, as a logical construct, needs to move away from the one-size-fits-all approach we have grown up with and into the realm of an omnipresent system that functions differently depending on the scenario, context, and desired outcome. Futurist Ray Kurzweil gave a 2014 TED Talk that helped us see a future where search works more like the human brain. He has spent years modeling the brain using ever more sophisticated brain imaging such as MRIs and electroencephalography (EEGs). This means that we can now peer more closely into the workings of the brain, with the goal of someday being able to replicate its functions in computing systems. Kurzweil explained his current theory on the brain's workings by walking his audience through an example of how we recognize the word "apple." He contends that our brains have hundreds of millions of what he calls *recognizers*:

- One recognizer sees the crossbar of the letter "A."
- Once that happens, the brain passes a signal up to the next levels of recognizers to confirm it is an "A." The same model occurs with P and L, using their respective characteristics.
- The information is then passed up to another, higher-level set of recognizers that determine that APPL is looking a lot like APPLE.
- The higher-level brain calls down to the part of the brain that can recognize "E" and asks it if what the visual system is seeing is likely an "E" at the end of the character set.
- If those lower-level recognizers say, "Yep, it's likely an 'E'," then the brain says that word is APPLE.

Of course, this all happens in nanoseconds. But that complex interplay of systems in the brain, each element of which has discrete functions that are subservient to the higher-order functions that govern our cognition, shows us what search has the potential to be.

If we think of search in this way—as a collection of systems with varying levels of capability—we can begin to project what is possible. This is a massive change for society. The billions of us who use search today would have to retrain ourselves to think of the experience and potential of search differently. When we first launched Bing, we asked users, "How conscious is your choice of search engine?" The results were astounding. People used the same amount of cognition in their choice of search engine that they did when deciding to brush their teeth at night or when they tapped their leg in a meeting, which is to say not very much. And while the question concerned brand preference, the implication is stark: people have been trained to search in certain ways and to expect certain things from search. Users don't query search engines with, "I wonder if there are stars any closer than Alpha Centauri" because they think, based on past experience, that the engine will fail. So even though the web is more capable, and search is rapidly becoming more capable, people don't yet think of it that way. And given the low cognitive energy people expend when deciding how to search, this isn't likely to change in the near future.

The alternative, and the one that seems more achievable, is to ask the producers of these systems to set them up to act more like the human brain, and to build discrete experiences and capabilities into things that *we already use*. Rather than asking several billion people to think about how to use search differently, maybe the best way is to not make them search at all...

Getting from Here to There

How do we create search systems that work more like the human brain? In the short term at least, there must still be a stimulus to get the engines to wake up and do something. Today, that stimulus is a search query. And to help bridge expectations, we should be building systems that allow a user to throw *anything* at an engine (speech, text, gesture, pictures, videos, and so on) and have the system return the most logical and helpful response given *what the person is trying to do, who he is,* and *the device he's using.*

This type of search, using any number of stimuli as a query, is imminently achievable today, even if the responses we get might not always be accurate, as our systems do not have all the connections to all the data that surrounds them and the models we've built to process the data aren't yet advanced enough to predict all outcomes with precision. Think about the previous chapter: we now have systems that have a great deal of information about the real world; let's call that "entity understanding." In addition to understanding entities, the systems understand the relationships between those entities. For example, systems know that a movie plays in a theater, a theater has showtimes, and moviegoers buy tickets to attend a showing; this is a stitching together of entities and information about those entities into something approximating knowledge.

The final component in the future of search—at least in the short term—is the introduction of action. Now that systems understand the real world, they are beginning to understand the actions that are possible. In search's near future, all these pieces—an understanding of everything in the world, the relationships among all these things, and how to interact with every person, place, or thing—will work in concert.

For example, if I want to volunteer at a spelling bee this weekend, search will:

- Know my location (from my social graph, because I recently checked in at a restaurant, or by using the GPS in my phone)
- Relate my location to an event (using an event graph, which associates meetings with physical locations) that occurs at a specific site (using the geospatial graph, which ties together named locations and GPS coordinates)
- Allow me to register as a volunteer via Meetup's registration service (using an action graph)

As you can see, the ability to link graphs is the key. Moving forward, search will be less about a "match" in the known-item retrieval model and more about the "blend" of all the signals and knowledge to which the search engine has access, so that it can help people navigate—either consciously or behind the scenes—and accomplish more of what they want to get done. Whereas search *was* about matching a request to a resource (usually a page, a picture, or a video) that existed on the web, weighted by how relevant the engine thought the page was to your search query, the new model is about taking these resources on the web and dynamically mashing them together in response to a *stimulus*. In other words, the new search is not about simple retrieval, but rather about constructing a specific cascade of information and actions that might not exist *anywhere* on the web. For example, there is no page on the web called "Stefan wants to volunteer at a spelling bee." There are pages and resources on the web that, when combined, can effectuate that task, but to do that requires much more than simply pulling up a page.

The Next-Generation Search Query

As we've said, nothing happens in search without some sort of stimulus. But what we think of as a stimulus needs to change. Formerly, a stimulus was a query you entered into a search box. Now a stimulus could be leaving your house, waking up on a Tuesday in Hong Kong, or spending $100 at Macy's. Even now, in systems like Google Now and Microsoft's Cortana, the stimulus is no longer a keyword but rather a *change in state*.

So what will happen when systems begin to work on your behalf without you taking explicit action? If a bar is too loud, for example, the system could alert you to move to the bar next door; the system knows you're on a first date with that person you met on Tinder, and devices in the bar next door report it's much quieter there.

For real magic to happen, systems have to be able to take a stimulus and act on it in a way that is in line with the user's ultimate goals. Thus the new search becomes less about what you want explicitly ("I want to find funny cat pictures") and more about giving the system a goal ("I want to laugh") and letting it figure out what makes the most sense, taking into account your personal preferences, your device, and the actions you can likely engage in right now given how much time you have, your location, and the likelihood you can pay attention under current conditions.

A Better Listener: Making Sense of the Nonsense

Speech recognition has gotten very, very good, in part because of higher-quality algorithms but also because of deep neural networks (DNNs). Without going into too much detail, DNNs attempt to model the human brain in the way they process data, making systems more flexible and less rule based. That, added to the fact that devices like your smartphone are nearly always connected, means the recognition can happen off the device and in massive server farms where the analysis task is distributed across hundreds of processors, not just the one or two on your phone, greatly enhancing both the speed and quality of the translation from sound wave to text.

Once we can convert the sound wave into text, the real challenge kicks in: trying to understand what that mass of words you just uttered actually means. Today, many systems are rule-based systems, meaning they use rules to map words (and collections of words) into concepts. We have gotten very far using this approach—at Bing we have systems like our entity repository. If someone says "Houston Rockets," we can look to our entity repository and see the person is talking about something classified as a sports team, in particular a U.S. basketball team (thank you, graph linking!). What the system actually sees is the word "Houston" and the word "Rockets"; it knows that when these two words occur in close proximity the speaker is probably talking about the basketball team. This works well with nouns but verbs are a little more complicated. The system can still technically recognize the verbs, but the question is what to do with them? Just because we can translate the sound wave into "Buy tickets" doesn't mean search has any idea how to fulfill the request.

Another challenge is that natural language can be ambiguous and often arbitrary. It doesn't translate easily to symbolic computer code, where there is no confusion about what a variable means. In symbolic language, "height" always means "height." It isn't also "tall" or "lanky" or "squat." Because of the ambiguous nature of language, it is very easy for a system to misinterpret input when applying a rule-based approach. In other words, if we rely on looking up words against known systems like our entity repository, we run the risk of misunderstanding the request. And while there are certainly many scenarios we can program into rules, the challenge is in handling a request when we have no rule for it. Today, systems fail pretty badly—services like Siri and Google Now simply throw your request to web search if they can't make sense of it.

In Focus: PARLANCE

Some exciting work has come out of a European Commission–funded project called PARLANCE (Probablistic Adaptive Real-Time Learning and Natural Conversation Engine), which has as its goal a search system that learns organically about the world rather than applying a rules-based approach. In essence, the system is like a child—it is born with a little framework, but as it interacts with its user, it gets things right but also makes mistakes. It corrects based on human interaction and it continually adds to its understanding of the real world. In other words, the system doesn't draw from a static dictionary that describes the world; instead, it uses its errors and successes to either correct or confirm its knowledge of the world.

What is most exciting about this development is the profound impact it will have on making search more personal. Today, rule-based systems cater to all manner of potential synonyms for a word (for example, some systems will do things like map the verb "watch" in the context of a movie application to "start, see, play, show, pull up," etc.).

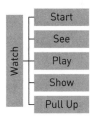

FIGURE 2-1

You can see the problem with this approach—first, if the word I generally use when I want to watch a movie is "view" and it isn't in the known list, the system fails. Moreover, I may never use words like "pull up" to start a show, so why should the system even have that as an option? All that does is increase the number of possible terms the system has to look through for every single query, raising the likelihood that it guesses incorrectly, as there are more potential terms from which to choose. With systems like PARLANCE, search can be completely tuned to the user. When a system has learned the particular words I use, my requests to go to *my* dictionary rather than to the same general language dictionary, greatly increasing the odds that it will get my request right.

Listening Harder

Even with intelligence of the type displayed by PARLANCE (described above), search systems that listen are still going to fail. A lot. Think about your human interactions. When you have a conversation, there is inevitably a back-and-forth that sets context, refines ambiguities, and truly engages both parties. So when I walk into a bar and yell out, "Landing gear!" you would expect that patrons would start asking refining questions (and perhaps wonder if I'd had too much to drink): "What do you mean by 'landing gear?' Are you asking about the landing gear on an airplane?" "Is that a drink?" "Is that the name of a bar you're looking for?" and so on. Once we'd reached an understanding—in this case let's say Landing Gear is a cocktail—there would be more refinement. "Do you want the bartender to make one?" "Are you asking what's in a Landing Gear?" "Are you wondering what the flavor is?" You get the idea. In human conversation, we use refinements to understand each other.

Imagine if, when I walk into the bar and yell out, "Landing gear," people just start throwing responses back. One person might quote me Wikipedia, another might start making the noise that landing gear makes when touching down, another might show me a video of a plane landing. It would be chaos. But that is exactly what happens with search today. Putting a search query into a modern search engine—especially if the words used are ambiguous—yields a Jackson Pollock–type approach to the answer. The system will splatter you with everything it knows about the words you entered: pictures, news, videos, maps, shopping sites, etc. And if one of those results isn't what you're looking for, you have to go back and try your query again.

Conversational understanding in search tries to bridge the gap between the system's first response to your query and what you were actually asking (since your first query may not have contained enough information to give you a suitable response. In systems like Microsoft's Cortana for the Windows Phone, you can ask questions in natural language, such as, "I'd like some good Mexican food near my house," and the system will engage in a dialog. You can ask follow-ups like, "Which of those are vegetarian?" Then say, "Okay, which ones take reservations?" And finally, "Which is the closest to me, and can I walk there?" At each stage, the system understands that you are referring to the previous interaction—it doesn't lose the context from one moment to the next, and it engages to better understand what you want.

Conversational understanding is critical to being able to do more with search, especially on devices without a great display and keyboard. Imagine trying to deal with keyword search on Google Glass or having to page through results on a one-line bracelet display. The future of search is going to be largely hands free; or at least there will be minimum of attention required, and yet you'll be able to accomplish substantial tasks. Today, we have to make far too many compromises when using non-PC device search, and we certainly aren't performing long research tasks on small screens with poor input methods. Having a system converse with you, actively alert you, and be able to respond naturally is the last piece of the puzzle. There are glimmers of this system intelligence today in Google Now and Cortana, and as more people begin to interact with them and the systems begin to consume more of the world's data, their powers of conversation and prediction will increase. None of the new capabilities of search can be fully exploited as long as we are engaging in caveman dialog with a system that

> Conversational understanding turns our search systems into participants rather than servants.

constantly forgets what you are talking about (although maybe this *is* a very human mode—at least that's what my girlfriend tells me).

Listening Smarter

Our ability to communicate with search engines using different devices is being enhanced every day. Whereas in the past we were constrained to mouse and keyboard, today's devices allow us to engage with search systems in more natural ways. Thanks to clever hardware and software designers, devices can be always listening or seeing, and are rapidly becoming smart enough to recognize when you are talking or interacting with them rather than with your wife.

- Moto X, the Android smartphone by Motorola, is a great example of an actively aware device. This phone listens constantly for the wake-up phrase "Okay, Google Now," which kicks it into search mode. In the past, there was entirely too much battery consumed when a device was always listening, but the engineers at Motorola developed new silicon that makes long activity periods possible without killing the device by 3 p.m.
- Gesture is also becoming a first-class input. The Xbox One, in addition to being able to turn on and navigate millions of titles without you ever touching a controller, allows you to use your body to interact with the system via its Kinect accessory. People often reference the movie *Minority Report* as a model for controlling computing interfaces—they picture themselves zipping around virtual interfaces like Tom Cruise, using nothing more than their hands. We certainly aren't there yet (and there is some question whether we want to be), but that possibility is in sight.

- Finally, better microphones and cameras, as well as advancements in digital signal processing, enable devices that are smart enough to understand when you are addressing them rather than someone else. The Ivee hardware assistant, a voice-controlled hub for smart homes, is constantly listening and you can activate it from anywhere in a room just by calling its name. Microsoft Research has a robot that directs visitors to the office of the person they are there to see, but only engages with the visitor when it is clear from her posture and gaze that she is speaking to it (the machine doesn't begin harassing passersby).

The bottom line? Our new search systems will have to "listen" to all manner of inputs, not just text and voice, and begin to synthesize them in order to make sense of our natural human interactions.

Understanding the Real World

In previous chapters we talked about how the world is being flooded with sensors and data that provide machines with a better understanding of the world in which they exist. But as we know, data is only the first step on the way to wisdom. In order for systems to live up to their potential, they must be grounded in the realities and constraints of the physical world. It's all well and good if a machine can calculate the exact time of sunrise and sunset at a particular location, but turning that calculation into an action—such as turning on your daughter's bedroom light so she isn't scared to go upstairs after dark—or a recommendation—such as telling you to leave your house now to catch the elusive "green flash" in the sky when the sun sets—is where the real potential lies. This conversion of information into intelligence and action paves the way for our systems to become our allies. And for that to happen, we need more than accurate times—we need what those times *mean* to us.

Helping People Help Search Engines Understand Them

One of the biggest challenges users have with search is phrasing queries in a way that tells the system what they are looking for. Once search systems have knowledge of the world they are able to help people form questions more effectively.

Think about doing something you haven't done before. Often you will seek out experts, or at least others who have experience in that area, so you can learn what questions you should be asking and so you can explore the topic fully. To get search to respond most effectively, you have to give it lots of hints about the thing you are looking for, which is hard if you don't have the vocabulary to describe your quest accurately. If you are setting out to buy a new camera, for example, you won't know which camera features are important unless you have done your research. Megapixels, sensor size, optical zoom, weight, charging cable type—these are all critical to making a good choice. But if you have never thought about buying a camera before, you won't know which factors are critical and which don't matter. When you search, you might type in a phrase like "best digital camera" and be led to a number of pages that feature reviews. Over time, you would learn what these experts think makes a good camera. You might discover that the most important things are the number of megapixels and the size of the sensor. Now, you would be able to search in a way that it would yield better responses for you.

Query formulation is one of the most challenging areas of our current search systems. You may type in a query, not get the result you want, and then scan the page of results for other words that might be helpful in retrieving the right resource from the index. Major search systems still see 25 percent or more of queries failing for users, as measured by how quickly users click back to the search results page after they have clicked on a link. In other words, one out of every four times people search, they formulate a query, don't find the information they want, and hit the back button to try a different combination of words.

> Major search systems still see 25 percent or more of queries failing for users.

When systems understand the real world better, there will be many more contextually helpful suggestions to standard queries. Rather than the hunt and peck of today's search, the near-term interfaces will be much smarter about understanding your likely meaning before you even hit "enter." Imagine that as you start typing "camera," the engine is already moving in the background, getting ready to show you attributes you might care about when it comes to selecting a camera. For example, it could prompt you to narrow down the type you're talking about—SLR or point-and-shoot?—with some helpful text explaining the difference.

In its simplest manner, search would just be reading from its knowledge index. It would know cameras have lots of characteristics, and would learn from user interactions which of these characteristics might be the most important. As the system continues to learn about the world, queries might be helped along by questions posed by the search engine, like, "Do you do lots of shooting in low light?" Again, if you weren't familiar with cameras or never had one before, you would likely not even think about low-light shooting, even though it's very important to get that piece of the buying decision right.

Devices Drive the Need for Understanding

Systems' ability to suggest what you might need to know in order to ask your question becomes more important as more of the world moves to mobile devices and the next generation of search. Part of the reason search hasn't progressed very far past its origins is that we've been spoiled with really good interaction vehicles, namely keyboards and big screens. When you can type a phrase quickly on a keyboard, hit "enter," and get results in under a second, the penalty for being sloppy or uneducated about your searches is fairly low. You simply hit "back" and key in a couple of different words.

On mobile devices or on devices with no screens or touch-interaction models, the penalty suddenly becomes much higher. Pecking out a long query on a mobile device keyboard, hitting search, and waiting the two or three seconds for results adds greatly to the time a user must spend with search to complete the simplest of tasks. The ability to augment a search query as the person is entering it (in whatever form the device enables) is critical to making search more helpful on these soon-to-be dominant devices. Of course, there will be tough issues and important considerations in the design of the user experience—the last thing anyone wants is Clippy, the now-defunct Microsoft Office Assistant, asking if you're trying to find a bus as you interact with search. The world's more helpful search systems will have to successfully blend real-world understanding with different search models in order to help people make the most of the changing web and the search it requires.

Today, we use search to win bar bets about what year *Flashdance* came out, but tomorrow search will help us tap into the near-infinite knowledge of the web and supplement our understanding of our world—not just how to find the answers but how to think about the questions. When search becomes less about "finding" or even "doing" and more about augmenting our limited individual knowledge of the world, we'll have a new superpower.

Building a Map of the World's Knowledge

Wolfram Alpha, a computational knowledge engine, debuted several years ago with the goal of allowing people to ask natural language questions and get answers based on data collected and synthesized from around the web. If you ask Wolfram Alpha something like, "What was the temperature in Detroit when 'Heat Wave' was released?" or "What is the cost of living in Boston versus Sacramento?" or "Number of car accident deaths per year?" or "Time between the Sputnik launch date and decay date?" the engine generates beautiful answers that not only respond to the question but also highlight additional sets of information from other linked graphs. For example, on the Sputnik question, note what else Wolfram "knows" about the timeframe surrounding the event. (See Figure 2-2 on the following page.)

Systems like Wolfram Alpha have done a great job of capturing and synthesizing data about the real world. But, as we have said, the truly exciting capacity of search is that it will do more than find things, it will get things done in the real world. To that end, Wolfram launched in March 2014 two even more ambitious projects—Wolfram Language and Wolfram Connected Devices. A full discussion of these projects is outside the scope of this book, but they are important for a couple of reasons.

First, Wolfram is offering the ability for people to write programs using the computational models he's built. Today one can ask millions of questions of the Wolfram Alpha engine, and now a developer will be able to write a program that takes advantage of that vast data bank to augment his

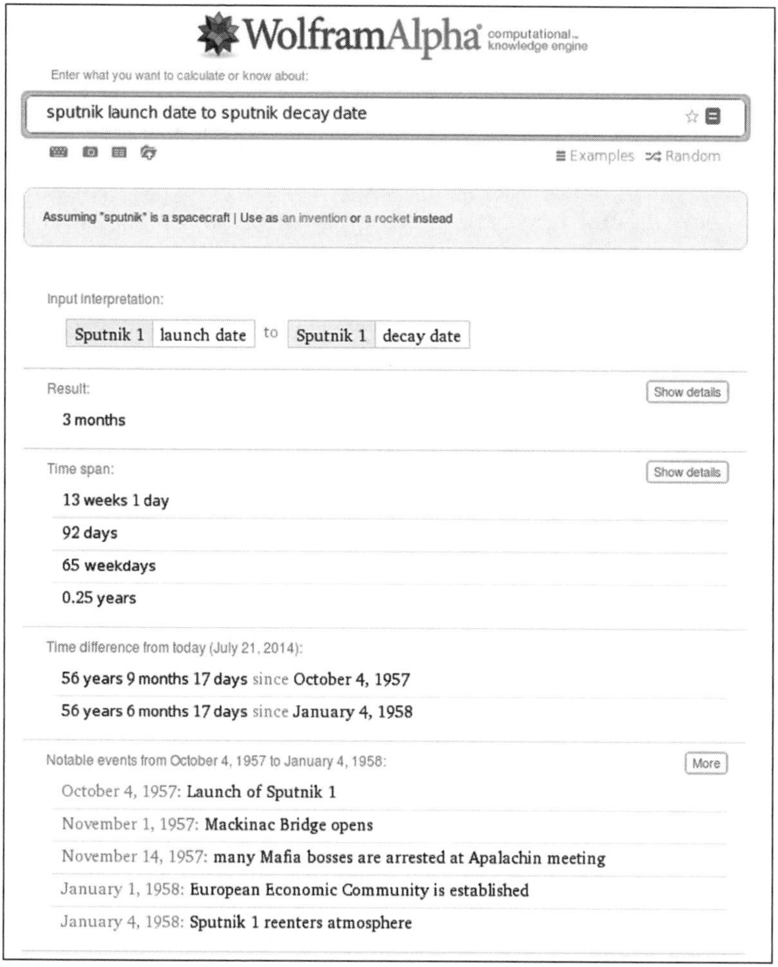

FIGURE 2-2

application. It's hard to get one's head around it, I admit, but the four thousand–plus functions in Wolfram Language enable you to do things like take historical weather data collected from sensors in cities and combine it with data on errors committed by a baseball team (along with hundreds of other variables)—and from that data you could derive a killer fantasy sports application. The potential result is similar to what we've spoken about earlier—that noisy devices and services (including weather stations, stats-tracking services, and more) are contributing massive amounts of disconnected data to the web. Systems like Wolfram allow anyone to stitch these pieces of data together to make intelligence from the noise.

Second, Wolfram isn't just a great information repository. One of the most intriguing parts of the system is its inherent ability to apply a knowledge layer on top of the data, so that we can not only pull information quickly from an index, we can leverage the system's capacity to make sense out of what might otherwise be simply one piece in a mass of data. For example, querying Wolfram on "legal paper vs ledger paper" yields a plethora of information about the two paper sizes

Input interpretation:
    US letter (paper format) | legal (paper format)

Basic properties   [show Metric] [More]

	US letter	legal
width	8.5 inches	8.5 inches
height	11 inches	14 inches
diagonal	13.9 inches	16.4 inches
aspect ratio	17 : 22 (1 : 1.29)	17 : 28 (1 : 1.65)
pixel count at 72 pixels/in	0.4847 megapixels	0.6169 megapixels
pixel count at 300 pixels/in	8.415 megapixels	10.71 megapixels
raw memory at 72 pixels/in	1.45 MB (megabytes) (24–bit)	1.85 MB (megabytes) (24–bit)
raw memory at 300 pixels/in	25.2 MB (megabytes) (24–bit)	32.1 MB (megabytes) (24–bit)

FIGURE 2-3

culled from a variety sources, and the system also displays calculated (or synthetic) characteristics that don't necessarily exist in other descriptions. So Wolfram tells us that legal paper can hold 10.71 megapixels of information at 300 pixels per inch (or about 32.1 MB worth of data).

Why is this interesting? Earlier, I used as an example my desire to volunteer at a spelling bee and noted that there was no web page for "Stefan wants to volunteer at a spelling bee." Search had to synthetically stitch together a number of unique pieces of data and services to resolve that query. Our legal versus ledger paper example shows similar profound implications. The ability to blend trillions of pieces of data and then look at those blends from different angles means that a system can do what we want to do naturally, which is stitch together things we know about in different domains to create an entirely new, helpful piece of knowledge. For example, I know that the higher in the atmosphere I go, the greater the amount of radiation I am exposed to. I also know that airplanes fly in the lower atmosphere as they whisk me across the world. A desire to understand how much radiation I am exposed to as I travel from New York to Seattle is a very human trait. The ability for systems to have access to this level of deduction is at the heart of understanding and interacting with our world, enabling search to serve as the bridge between what we know and what we desire to know.

Both Google and Bing are also building systems that aim to "re-create" the entire world inside their systems. Bing's entity repository stores billions of descriptions of real-world objects and the connections between them, and it adds millions more every month; Google's Knowledge Graph does much the same. Having search systems understand the real world rather than simply the pages on the web gives us the opportunity to make search functional rather than just informational.

CHAPTER 3

What Search Will Do

When search has access to and better understands the world in which it operates, the result is not greater access to information "stored" on the web. As we have seen, the capable web is not a static store from which we can draw, but is instead a hot soup of trillions of micro-sized characterizations of the real world. Some of these characterizations manifest in the classic web pages we've come to expect from the Internet, whereas others are more latent and transitory ("likes" and location data, for example), and still other characterizations enable systems to manipulate the real world. Once we get our heads around the new tapestry that is the web and think through the way search will have both access to it and the ability to participate in its creation (rather than just retrieve from it), we can glimpse a future of what search will actually *do*.

Search Will Be Insightful and Predictive

The next generation of search depends in part on the ability of the system to not only compute characteristics of the real world, but to apply those computations and predict what might happen next. That could mean telling you when to leave for home to beat the traffic that comes with a baseball game in town tonight or it could mean alerting you to a news story that might affect your financial picture.

There has been no shortage of articles written about the power of "big data" and its ability to inform decision making in personal and business situations—in essence, the capacity to derive insights from a system's understanding of the world. Many of us have heard the story from a few years ago about Target using the purchase history of a customer to discern that she was likely pregnant, and sending a piece of direct mail offering baby registry services to the address on file. The problem? The father who opened the mail at the house was furious at Target for sending the solicitation, because certainly no one in the house was pregnant. Guess what? His teenage daughter was. Target's ability to look for patterns (people who bought certain things over a specific time period were likely pregnant) is what makes people both excited and nervous about the power of data. In this case, Target's system was both highly insightful and dramatically predictive in that it used purchase data tied to its loyalty card to derive an insight (someone was pregnant) and predict a future action (she will soon need to buy diapers).

What are some of the other possibilities open to us if we begin to fuse unlikely data sets together to create a search experience that offers insights, not just answers? One of the most interesting studies was conducted by Eric Horvitz, who holds both an MD and a PhD in computer science and is past president of the Association for the Advancement of Artificial Intelligence (AAAI). He had a hypothesis that search wasn't very good at handling certain types of time-sensitive queries. For example, you may need to know how to stop severe bleeding, help a baby who is choking, care for a person having an epileptic seizure, or perform CPR. The obvious time-sensitive queries were just that—obvious. "Having a heart attack" or "choking" were pretty simple to classify. But the beauty and challenge of search is that people can put in anything as a query. So how do we go about classifying queries that aren't immediately obvious? In this case, Horvitz analyzed query logs and identified chains of queries (basically a succession of queries within a period of time) in which the final query was something like a hospital address. He also looked at mobile query chains and isolated sets where the GPS stopped at a hospital or the user dialed 911. By tying together disparate graphs (location, phone, queries), he was able to train the system to better understand situations where an immediate response was necessary. Then, he made sure his team built responses that made sense given the query's urgency. For example, if search detected a query that was likely resolved by CPR, the system would not show a YouTube video on CPR that had a two-minute introduction by the county fire chief (even though it might be a great video). For a search conducted on a mobile phone, once the system detected a pattern of queries, it could automatically begin to build a route to the nearest hospital or dial 911 in the background.

In another example, feeds from Twitter enabled Horvitz's team to predict which women would likely suffer from post-partum depression. Using public tweets, the team was able to identify accounts belonging to new moms by employing a classifier (a fancy term for a system that organizes and finds patterns among data). The team would identify and confirm that a particular user had just had a baby by watching for phrases like, "Timothy Alex Smith, 7 pounds 2 ounces," and then they monitored the tweets after the user gave birth. The researchers took several hundred new moms, aligned according to the birth dates of their babies, and then looked at severe changes in affect in these people. They noticed significant changes in about 15 percent of the study group, a proportion that aligns with the postpartum depression rates in new moms. If that wasn't amazing enough, they then asked themselves: Can we go back three months before the birth of the child and attempt to figure out *which of these women are likely to have postpartum depression,* and then build a model to recognize high-risk women so they can get support before the birth? Guess what? They could.

People will point out that all this data still can't deliver to us the sort of sentience I've predicted for search systems. When human behavior and health are part of the equation, there is the question of nature versus environment and how those factors affect outcomes. In other words, you may be genetically predisposed to Alzheimer's because of a gene expressed in your DNA but that doesn't mean you will develop it. There are hundreds of factors in your environment that can mitigate or accentuate your risks. Certainly, we can't monitor all of them, and even if we could, the number of models that we could build—and the conflicting outcomes they may predict—would be limited.

So you could say that the risk of incorrectly predicting postpartum depression—because you've used less than complete data and guessed wrong—outweighs the potential benefit. But is that the case? As we've seen in previous chapters, the amount of data about the world that is collectible and actionable is exploding. It is true that models that predict disease based on genes would be flawed because *we can't collect all the environmental factors affecting a given person.* But what if we could? Suddenly, it's not only your genes that tell us you're likely to develop Alzheimer's; the fact that you live near an aluminum smelter and eat lots of fish loaded with mercury will also increase your likelihood. As we discussed in the previous chapter, all manner of environmental and personal factors can now be known, measured, and recorded to enable better predictions about what will happen, to whom, and when. Even more exciting, people can take advantage of this information to reduce the likelihood of something bad happening or increase the likelihood of something good happening. But how do we empower people with this kind of search? We will discuss this further in chapter 8.

Challenge: Insights Through Blind Curiosity

One of the challenges of building understanding into intelligent systems is that engineers need to know what exactly to build into them. We aren't yet at the point where systems are curious for curiosity's sake—they still have to be told what to look for. The types of searches humans construct come from a hypothesis that if a, then b. In other words, a system today won't, on its own, decide to look through all the solar flare data to determine whether cellular service is likely to be impacted. Certainly, a human who understands the correlation between solar activity and cell service can direct a computer to analyze the available data, but the hypothesis had to exist before the insight could be coded. We talked a little bit in chapter 1 about how a system at Google has begun to expand beyond the boundaries of its programming, but even that is incremental.

One of the solutions to the problem of machines being inherently incurious is to stop asking "Why?" As humans, we want to understand not just that something happened but the impetus behind it. It's not enough to understand someone died—we want to know *why* she died. It is why we do autopsies even though there is no chance that we can bring the person back (well, that and insurance payouts).

Dr. Horvitz gave me an example of how this lack of an initial hypothesis could be applied to learning systems. The last time he arrived in Beijing, he got into a cab with the intent of going to his hotel. Over the next several minutes, he tried using broken Chinese, hand gestures, and pictures to communicate with his driver. After much back and forth, the driver got on the road and ended up at the right place. Now, imagine if we could capture every interaction with every tourist and every taxi driver and the corresponding destination in Beijing. The system could build a model based on these particular utterances, pictures, and gestures, made in the presence of taxi drivers in Beijing, that interprets the person's likely destination as the Ritz-Carlton. In this case, the system doesn't need to understand the *why*, it just must recognize that this pattern of interaction in the presence of another human inside a taxi likely results in a particular destination. The temptation, of course, is to try to explain why this is the case—certainly, as humans, that is what we do—but the reality is we likely don't have to. Does it make search less human? Yes. Does it matter in this example? Probably not.

This is not to say that we should blindly accept correlation as we build our systems. Data scientists routinely point out that correlation is not the same as causation. You can show a correlation between the number of cell phones and CO_2 emissions in a country (data reveals that the more cell phones there are, the higher the emissions). However, it is unlikely there is a causal link between the two. No one really believes that more cell phones *cause* increased CO_2 emissions; rather, the two variables are simply correlated. In another example, Facebook recently posted a hilarious response to a Princeton study purporting to show that Facebook will lose 80 percent of its users in the next two years. Applying the same methods the study used to show Facebook's decline, Facebook showed Princeton would be empty of students by 2021; again, correlation and causation were confused.

Remember: correlation is not causation.

Enough Is Enough?

Improvements to search are also enhancing the system's ability to derive insights and make predictions by recognizing the point at which it's no longer useful to collect information. Much academic research has been done to understand at what point a decision should be made in a search system, given that data is constantly streaming in from all sources. The system has to constantly ask, "Is there enough information to understand what is happening and offer a statistically accurate prediction, or is more data necessary? And further, if more data is collected, is there a possibility that the prediction won't be any better or could actually yield a worse result because of the delay?"

I'm reminded here of the aphorism, "The perfect is the enemy of the good." In other words, a person (or a search system) could collect data on an event forever and never make a decision. That obviously won't work in search; but we also need to make sure we have *enough* information to feed the predictive models on which this next generation of search relies. The computer science behind these models is far beyond the intellectual capacity of this author, but we can examine a layperson's view of the challenge by looking at a traffic and routing scenario.

A search engine may get information from a traffic and navigation application like Waze about an accident on your route home. The question for the engine is whether it should tell you immediately or wait to tell you. If the system waits, it could potentially gather other information to validate whether the accident is causing an issue. It may be that the accident is minor and has already been moved off the road, thus causing no material day in your commute home. But if the system doesn't wait around to gather that additional data, and instead advises you as soon as an alert of the accident comes in, it may reroute you to a path that ultimately takes you far longer than if you had stayed on the road where the minor accident occurred.

The system must balance the advantages and disadvantages of dispensing information quickly—it must reach a certainty threshold that the information is good and its predictions are true, and that the decisions it makes ultimately give you the optimal outcome. By waiting for additional information that shows the severity of the accident, the system could create a delay that pushes you past the point where there are other routing options, thus dooming you to a lengthy commute home. There is no perfect answer here—systems will make errors, just as humans do when deciding when it's best to give someone information. As researchers continue their study and as the additional digital fidelity of the real world is consumed by engines, the ability of those systems to know the optimal time to trigger an event will increase.

From Finding to Doing

Search needs hands and feet to actually accomplish things in the real world. While we are making great progress in getting search systems to understand the world, understanding without the ability to take an action hampers the true potential of search. That's where applications come in.

As of early 2014 there are more than 1.5 million apps across the various operating systems of our devices. There could very well be more, but vendors are notoriously quiet about their numbers. These applications enable us to do things like:

- Waste time (hello, Angry Birds!)
- Record a conversation for later
- Manage our travel schedules
- Make payments

- Track our finances
- Hail a cab
- Book hotels
- Capture a moment
- Control lights and appliances in our homes

In short, the application explosion lets our smart devices augment our natural abilities as humans. To take a simple example: I want to get a cable for my phone delivered to me but I am in meetings for the entire day. What were my options before the advent of services like Postmates and Task-Rabbit? I could call a friend (hard to do in a meeting), hope I have an assistant with a car whom I can e-mail, or make a note to myself to pick one up on the way home. In all cases, the inefficiency of the task—finding someone who can help me, and owing that person a favor and remembering that for the future, or having to stop on the way home and park in a garage, just so I can get a silly cable for my phone—not only crushes my productivity but adds cognitive load to my already overburdened mind.

Today, what are my options? I can launch one of several apps that enable me to source a person (who is at that time underutilized from a production standpoint) to go wherever I need him to go, buy the cable, and drop it off wherever I want. I tell the system what I am willing to pay, and if someone finds the amount worth his time, he accepts the job. That person handles going to the store, finding the cable, and purchasing the cable. Once he has dropped the cable off at the place I have specified, an alert comes to my app, including the amount I owe for both the task and the cable, and, with a single tap, I pay the bill. And this can all be done without me ever saying a word; I can execute the entire operation from my phone held under the conference table as others in the meeting drone on about quarterly projections.

Pushing Beyond the "Appocalypse"

Applications and the functions they can perform on my behalf are, however, an interim step to achieving the goal of having search do things for me. My core question is this: Why the heck should I have to install an app to figure out what time the subway comes to the Second Avenue stop in New York City? Or to identify the constellation I'm looking at in the sky? Or to calculate the tip at a restaurant? Many of these "applications" are really nothing more than a query to one or more structured data sources wrapped in a user experience that makes it easy to operate on a device. Think about it: there is nothing as inelegant as me having to say, "I wish I could take the subway to Rockefeller Center, so I think I'll hang out here on the corner in twenty-one-degree weather and search an application marketplace on my teeny little keyboard and small screen using a keyword search from 1994 and hopefully stumble across some piece of code I can download over a congested cellular network and install in my limited local storage that, by the way, will consume battery life as it turns itself on to receive push notifications I don't need, all so I can figure out if it's the F or D line I need to take north."

Appocalypse: Too many apps that are too hard to find.

The saner approach pushes "apps" to search—this is key to realizing the "action" portion of search. Rather than requiring an explicit indication of intent on the part of the user (i.e., I install an app because I need the subway map), engines should detect implicit intent. When I query for Rockefeller Center and I'm sitting at the Thompson Hotel on Manhattan's Lower East Side, a logical intent is that I want to travel to Rockefeller Center. The magic will be in mapping derived intent onto a new lightweight model of "apps" that are little more than a bunch of published capabilities on the web.

Less geeky: imagine a bunch of applications in the cloud that are waiting for a search engine to call on them and ask them for information or whether they can do something in the real world. In the above example, my query for subway lines from where I am on the Lower East Side to Rockefeller Center triggers the engine to ask the most reputable "subway app" in the cloud for that information, get the information from the app, and display it in the search response.

The idea that search should understand what apps can do and employ their capabilities in response to a query isn't wholly new. Some quick history: UDDI (Universal Description Discovery and Integration) was basically a big directory in the sky where web services could register themselves so applications knew which web service they should use to, for example, authorize a credit card. UDDI is dead and gone but the idea is still magnificent—indeed, it's more relevant today than it was in 2000 when it was conceived. Because now, with nearly 1.5 million apps (many of which are disguised web services), all but the savviest consumers are more confused than ever about how to do stuff on the web.

So what do we need? A few things:

• **A way to register app capabilities:** We need the ability for apps to register their interfaces and methods. For those with less technical backgrounds, this means we need applications to publish in a structured format the type of information they have, what they can do, how they should be queried, and how they will respond to the asker. The apps would publish this to a directory in the cloud.

• **Micropayments:** Information and services aren't free, and we shouldn't expect companies or individuals to curate information or offer a physical service for nothing. Today, I pay $1.99 for an application for the subway map. Moving forward, there must be some way to charge the engine or the user for access to the information. Micropayments would be far less expensive than individual apps—likely fractions of a cent for information like subway routing.

• **Persistent login and accounts:** Having to constantly log in and choose the right account associated with a service is also a barrier to seamless app capability brokering. Today, there is no way for people to easily micropay for information from apps that aren't funded by existing models of advertising. A persistent login and single identity would also reduce the system's incorrect selection of an app, as it would more carefully tune intent models to individual users.

• **Ratings:** Part of selecting the appropriate application for an intent is knowing which is "best." Systems can use ratings for explicit learning, and an evolution of good old machine learning will help systems understand implicitly which apps to load based on how often the particular apps result in users being able to complete a task.

How is an understanding of the capabilities of the millions of applications available to us relevant to search? Expanding on the earlier example of my need for a charging cable: I realize I have forgotten my phone's charging cable at my house. I am at the office, and am leaving for a trip later in the afternoon. I have no time to go home or to the store. What to do? Today, I query the web or people I know and ask them what I should do. One of these sources may tell me that there are two apps that provide delivery services—TaskRabbit and Postmates. I go to my phone and install the app, then conduct the transaction, including having to register with the service, set up a payment method, learn how to use the service, and ultimately navigate the app. This is still not very efficient. The real thing I want to do—my intent—is get a cable delivered to me before I leave on my trip.

I should be able to simply tell search I need a cable for my phone before I leave for the airport, and search should take the following steps:

- Examine the phone model from which I am issuing the request (something done all the time today)
- Derive my intent (that I need to buy a cable)
- Figure out the constraints (I need it before my calendar says I am on a plane, minus the time the system predicts it will take me to get to the airport and check in)
- Determine which services on the web can fulfill my request
- Issue a request to the app using a defined set of information (requester, delivery address, amount the requester is willing to pay [derived either from my personal profile or the average price for a delivery task reported by the service], what the task is, and when it needs to be completed)

Lest you think this sounds too much like science fiction, I would point you to the web documentation for the API (application programming interface) for the TaskRabbit service, which would allow a system like the one described above to be built and to accomplish of these action-based steps today.

The current challenge—which search companies are working on—is that there is no consistent way for a search engine to understand what apps there are, what they can do, and how to talk to them. It's as though you are shopping in a bazaar in Istanbul and you think there is likely a place you can buy saffron, but finding it and then communicating with the stall owner in your native language makes any transaction incredibly difficult. You have neither an understanding of the options available to you nor the ability to talk with the stall owner to find out whether you can get what you want given your conditions—when you need it, how much you can pay, and so on. This is the state of search and applications today.

In Focus: An Action-Based Web

I remember the first time I used the Siri application, long before Apple acquired the technology. It was back in 2009, and I installed it on an iPhone 3G while walking with my daughter to a play. After the application finished installing, I told it, "I'm looking for a romantic restaurant in Austin next Tuesday for two at 7:30." Within a few seconds Siri responded with a list of restaurants that Yelp reported as being romantic and OpenTable reported as having availability, and asked me if I wanted to book one of them. It was amazing—it literally listened to me, understood what I was trying to do, and then used appropriate web resources to turn my intent into action. We're still not back to that point, though it was five years ago (Apple made some changes for scale and global adoption), but that experience showed me the first glimmer of what search can be, combining knowledge, insights, and action.

Recently there have been attempts from services like EverythingMe and Quixey to track the apps that exist for a given need. For example, you can query Quixey with, "Find a local doctor," and the system will return multiple applications that let you find and book a doctor near your location. So we are making progress—this solves the problem of discovery at a human level, because now I can find and install an application that helps me complete a task. The next iteration, obviously, is to build a system that can find information and services, interrogate the services and their capabilities, and ultimately use that information to help you do something in the real world.

You can see some of this potential on modern smartphones from Google, Apple, and Microsoft. Telling your phone to "Find me the closest hospital" or "Send a text to my girlfriend" invokes applications on the device that handle the request. For requests like texting a certain person, systems like Siri have been hardcoded so that, once the system detects your intent (albeit in a pretty crude way), there isn't a ton of ambiguity about which app to launch to fulfill the instruction, "Text my girlfriend." And if there is, you have a problem search likely can't solve.

Systems like Windows and Windows Phone are making great strides in suggesting apps in relation to what you're searching for. When I use Windows Phone to find a restaurant in a new city, I am presented with applications that could help me get a table or find parking nearby. Even more exciting, with Cortana on Windows Phone, when I land in a new city, the device suggests popular apps to help me get around and make the most of my time—without me ever asking.

Making Everything Smarter

Part of the next generation of search is the ability to access it wherever you may be. As devices get smaller and more capable, and arrive in forms that don't have a display or input method, we need them to think for themselves without relying on stimulus from a human.

It's important here to call attention to one more innovation from Wolfram that highlights how machines will be able to act on their own. Raspberry Pi is a $35 computer that has been programmed by tens of thousands of hobbyists and students to do just about anything a simple computer can do. If you can dream a task and put it into code, Raspberry Pi is the perfect, inexpensive kit to carry it out, whether you want your computer to turn on the coffeemaker, act as an Internet radio, or automatically control lights when you arrive at home. Other similar projects exist, including the Arduino (a $100 minicomputer), which has the ability to easily snap on custom hardware to do things like turn it into a 3D printer ($99), make it into a robot ($30 for a motor controller), or give it eyes, ears, and sensitivity to moisture ($15 + cameras and mics).

Today these devices run on simple programming languages, much like any other computer. However, Wolfram announced in 2014 that it is embedding the Wolfram Language into Raspberry Pi, meaning that suddenly a $35 computer has fairly advanced understanding and an ability to query and interact with the real world. Combine that with the inexpensive hardware add-ons that are being developed by people in the Arduino and Raspberry Pi communities, and you have a computer that can not only understand the real world but take action in it.

And taking action is where Wolfram's work comes in. Part of Wolfram's charge is to enable any device to talk to any other connected device. According to Wolfram: "Our goal is not just to deal with information about devices, but actually be able to connect to the devices, and get data from them—and then do all sorts of things with that data."

In other words, the company's goal is to build a database that details millions of devices, their capabilities (this device can extrude a piece of metal, this device can measure altitude, this device can measure body temperature), and how to talk to them, so every device on the planet can be connected into the global intelligence, powered in part by Wolfram's language (though ultimately we will likely see other languages as well).

What does all this mean? It means that it seems silly for search to refer to a crawler scouring web pages for information that can be returned when a person enters the right keyword and hits the match jackpot. When every device on the planet is talking in some way, and search systems know how to communicate with them, and the devices themselves understand their function and purpose in the real world, your search might consist of you pointing your phone at a screw you need to fix your antique dresser and having it copied by a 3D printer in your office. Or, if you injured your ankle while on a run, search might mean having your medical data read from your bracelet and sent to the nearest ER, which dispatches an ambulance to come get you.

No matter the scenario, the potential of devices to understand what they can do and what other devices around them can do—and to have a framework that allows them to talk and coordinate with each other—is profound when we think about how this work can connect the virtual with the real world, and how search can then truly be the hinge that connects the best of both worlds.

Devices Make Friends, Influence Each Other

It's one thing to have devices that can "think," but to truly achieve the potential of next-generation search, they need to be able to talk to each other. Companies in addition to Wolfram are now getting in on the game, working to develop an alliance that could power the "Internet of everything." The AllJoyn system, developed as an open source project from the AllSeen Alliance, is working with major manufacturers of devices on a set of standards that allows devices to talk to each other. Why? Today, even with all these signals coming from all these devices, there still has to be some translation layer so that each device knows what the other is saying, what it can do, and how to ask it to carry out tasks.

Having a standard language that devices use to express their capabilities and constraints would remove the need for translation and would eliminate potential mistranslations. That is good, because it is unclear that anyone is really building such a translator. And even if someone was, the business model is illusory because helping a light switch talk to a microwave seems like a problem that would be hard to monetize at scale. Not needing each device to talk to a cloud server to understand what another device is saying is also good for the overall system, as each layer or process introduces yet another failure point.

Other mechanisms, like SkyNet.im, offer a very simple framework for device-to-device communication—in essence, providing a way for everything from devices to sensors to servers to talk to one another. Today there is still a fair bit of programming involved in, for example, making a cheap motion sensor talk to three drones, but the goal of the group is to make such communication something people without computing experience can do using a simple drag-and-drop interface. The mission is for any device or system to be able to talk to any other, and we simply have to say to them, "If you see this, then do that." It's a beautiful interim step to the fully autonomous Internet of Things that will be able to take action without being explicitly told what to do.

For example, I still need to be explicit about programming my lights to come on when the front door opens and the motion sensor detects motion in the hall. There is also a very defined language each device in the house has to use in order to effect this level of orchestration. Systems like SkyNet.im give us the means to talk to anything, and have all the elements talk to one another. It is only a small leap to think that, with time, we will develop systems that allow these devices to learn the most logical actions to take given the conditions in which they find themselves,

Devices will be able to control themselves and one another.

meaning the lights come on when I arrive at home because it makes sense, not because I told a system they had to.

Bringing the Pieces Together

As we have seen up to this point, many parts of the next-generation search system are in development. Some pieces are being built very deliberately while others' purpose remains undefined. Marc Davis, a pioneer in human-computer interactions and developer of many intelligent systems, sees search as an orchestrator of these many parts, making it the key to building a truly predictive and useful hinge:

> The competition in search is going to come down to who can provide the most trusted platform environment and experience for the digital person to be empowered in the web of the world and by doing so, to have your life be the query.
>
> Keyword search is still useful at certain times, but really what you want is that your life is the query, and there's some nice examples of this. There's this notion called Ready the Hand—you think of people that work together really well. You're in an operating room, and the surgeon reaches out their hand and the scalpel appears without him or her having to ask for it because the partner in that process knows them so well and understands what's going on well enough that they don't have to request it. It just appears.
>
> They didn't have to ask when they reached out their hand, it's just suddenly the scalpel is there. I think what we're going to see in search is, as these technologies get better and the right privacy and permissions and data architectures emerge, the potential for information and services to be available proactively without your having

to ask for it is there because effectively living your life is the query. I think that potential is really profound.

Thus, your *life* becomes the stimulus for search. And search, because it knows you so well and can anticipate your needs even before you do, appears where you need it with the right answer, the right service, or the right piece of assistance. It does this by understanding you and the real world; it understands your patterns and how the things around you act and interact, and it is able to determine the best course of action to present to you as it constantly evaluates all potential scenarios and outcomes, discarding poor results and promoting optimal outcomes.

Can Next-Generation Search Increase Happiness?

It's an interesting paradox: because we are getting more and more data, one would assume we'd be able to predict anything, but that is not necessarily the case. It is logical to assume that with more data comes better search and better predictions. And given enough time and granularity, that is very true. When systems are confronted with *so* much data, though, certain types of queries, those for which one needs a response quickly, cannot be answered in a time frame that is acceptable to the searcher.

We humans have learned tricks to cope with all the vast amount of data around us—these experience-based techniques for finding solutions are known as *heuristics*. It's a well-accepted fact that we would lose our minds if we were forced to process all the visual, aural, and other sensory inputs that come to us from the real world. Heuristics are mental shortcuts that help us solve problems that might not be exactly equivalent to situations we've seen before, but which could probably be solved in a satisfactory, if not perfect, way by applying an "about right" model.

And we use heuristics not just because of the overwhelming number of inputs we face, but also because rationalizing our way through all the variables would likely make us obsess over every decision. Imagine trying to pick out a pair of shoes using the crushing level of detail our minds can hold. Not only would you have to find ones that optimally match your clothing (your socks, your belt, your pants and shirt—a staggering multivariate function), but you would then have to rationalize every other variable, including factors like: If they get wet will they stain? How much heel is left on the shoes? Are they easy to remove if I have to pass through security? And so on. This is just a sampling of the amazing number of considerations our brains could run through for every decision. You can see why heuristics are very important, as we're able to take all of these considerations and apply a "good enough" model that lets us quickly decide on shoes by using past experiences to generate an outcome that is likely going to resolve the conundrum to a decent level of satisfaction.

But here is the interesting question. Does this "sampling" or "good enough" approach to life mean that we are leaving significant potential for happiness on the table? Dr. Barry Schwartz, a professor at Swarthmore College, outlines this challenge in his seminal book *The Paradox of Choice,* in which he analyzes the correlation of too many choices with a decline in overall happiness. In other words,

> Does our reliance on heuristics mean we leave too much happiness on the table?

when a person is presented with many, many choices of laundry detergent, his happiness with his ultimate selection is lower than if he had only a couple of choices.

In addition, Nobel Prize winner Daniel Kahneman points to a risk of not knowing all the variables when making decisions, when he talks about one of the key challenges with heuristics. Kahneman introduces a concept he labels *What You See Is All There Is* (WYSIATI): in essence, when we make a decision, our mind only takes into account what it already knows or has observed in the past (what he calls *known knowns*). The challenge, of course, is that there are many, many variables that could affect the decision that the mind hasn't previously observed. Kahneman calls these *known unknowns*, and he theorizes that we aren't very good about thinking through those potentials without serious introspection (and certainly not when we make the quick decisions we must make hundreds of times a day). More worryingly, the mind completely ignores any possibility of *unknown unknowns*—things that are unobserved and whose relevance to the decision is unclear.

The point? Humans are not capable of truly taking in to account all the things they should consider when making decisions. Our world is a very complex one with trillions of variables acting on us at any given point in time. But because our minds are tuned to make decisions using known knowns, and that universe of observations is relatively small in comparison to the vast array of known unknowns and unknown unknowns, the chance of making an excellent decision in most situations is pretty rare. Last, we tend to assume chaos doesn't exist and we expect that our current situation will mirror the last one that looked like it. As we know from many mutual fund commercials, this likely isn't true.

That said, search *could* augment our abilities, in this age of overwhelming data, if we stop treating it as a one-size-fits-all system. In other words, if we're able to turn search into a generalizable broker that could, in parallel, run tens of millions of "what if?" scenarios and bubble up only that piece of information we really need to know or that action we need to take, our psyche just might benefit—at least according to the paradox of choice. But if we continue to think of search as simply a system that must in thirty milliseconds return a pithy response to a fragmented sentence that we enter into it, we run the risk of reinforcing the overwhelming cavalcade of choice presented to us in an increasingly complex web.

This notion is perhaps best summed up by Alfred North Whitehead, who observed, "Progress is measured by what you no longer have to think about." Once search understands the world, can participate in it via devices and services that allow it to understand and manipulate the physical world, and is able to augment our natural human abilities in both thinking and doing, the question of what search *will* "do" is less relevant than thinking about what search w*on't be able* to do.

Up to this point, we've mostly spoken about the systems that will make these new experiences possible. Thinking about how these search systems will show up in our everyday lives—how we will actually interact with and benefit from them—is the focus of the next chapter.

CHAPTER 4

What Search Will Be

Search, in its enlightened form, has the potential to be the hinge that finally connects humanity with machines in a way that lets us transcend our biological limitations. We are at a point in technical history where we have the pieces necessary to augment human abilities in ways that will give superpowers to those of us with access to these systems. The capacity to know anything that can be known and do anything anywhere in the world, no matter where your physical body lies, is as close to a reality as it has ever been.

Of course, the old joke, popular in technical circles, applies: "It has been the year of [insert hot technology here] every year for the last ten years." In other words, we technologists are terrible at predicting when technology hits a tipping point and jumps from science fiction or research to reality.

Indeed, right about now there are undoubtedly a good number of people who are reading this and saying, "So far you've described a data-driven technological utopia that looks and sounds impressive, but so did the Mechanical Turk." In nerd lore, the Mechanical Turk was a robotic chess player built in the late eighteenth century that traveled from expo to expo, challenging and beating chess players in towns across the world. In the end, however, the magic of an autonomous chess grandmaster was unmasked to be a person (a *really good* chess player) controlling pulleys and levers to give the robot an appearance of supreme intelligence.

What issues do we face in turning our version of Mechanical Turk into a fully able-bodied chess grandmaster? We alluded to some of them earlier, but we'll spend a little time here going into more detail about the challenges we must overcome in order to bridge the gap between machine and human abilities.

- **Impedance mismatch:** Machines can overwhelm us with information, while humans can demand too much in too little time.
- **Unfamiliar situations:** Machines today often fail or default to simple behaviors when confronted with a situation they aren't equipped to handle, while humans enter a situation and, in many cases, don't use the right information (or don't have the information) necessary to maximize benefit in the situation.
- **Lack of humanity:** Currently, machines can't fool humans into thinking they are other humans. This is the basis of the Turing Test held every year, in which systems compete to see which one can successfully hold a conversation with a human without the human knowing the other participant is a computer. So far, no computer has passed the test. It's certainly one explanation why, in systems like Siri or Cortana, 30 to 40 percent of all interactions people initiate are social or silly questions that probe the reality of the "assistant" rather than inquiries the system was intended to answer. We want (and need) to believe we're engaging with someone who understands not only math but our humanity.
- **Unclear authority:** We go to the doctor not to be presented with a list of a hundred palliative choices based on our diagnosis, but to get one or a few. We often follow

experts' advice because they are that—experts—and we believe we have some way to vet their credentials, whether by a designation at the end of their name or because they have proven themselves qualified in some other public sphere. Such trust in authority doesn't exist—and probably shouldn't—with today's search systems.

- **Analog rationality (or lack thereof):** We as humans enjoy the flexibility to not make sense if we choose. We can make decisions for reasons known only to us that may seem wonky to others around us. Machines today would struggle with this ability to do what seems contradictory to the most logical outcome.

There are many who believe that systems won't be able to truly simulate and augment human intelligence given the challenges noted. Noam Chomsky argues that science is inadequate or, more harshly, kind of shallow. He contends that even if we can teach a system to understand a basic concept like gravity and return results and images based on that query, we really haven't taught search what gravity means to the world.[1]

There has certainly been much written about how generalized artificially intelligent systems have failed to materialize. We have been working on AI concepts since the 1950s and AI systems since the '60s, and some would argue that we are still unable to succeed on fairly basic tests.

Chomsky asserts that the real progress we're seeing is in areas where there are simple systems. Physics, he maintains, is simple in that we can measure real-world things and make good progress. I would argue that there is merit to the idea, but I think there is another way of viewing the progress we will make with AI that both validates his argument and also undermines it: one of the reasons we do not have better AI is that *we have never had enough data* to model the real world. Imagine, ten years ago, trying to track the light levels in a room over the course of a day. You would have had to perch in a room all day long with a light meter and take measurements each hour, quarter hour, or minute, and you'd still be only fractionally as accurate as a $10 device today, which can measure and publish light levels at microsecond-long intervals.

In all cases, the *fidelity* of the measurements is increasing. The resulting resolution means it will soon be possible for systems to apply models to the data to understand interactions among the "invisible forces" all around us. Most of us don't understand why, for example, our computer speakers would buzz when we're about to get a text on an old Motorola phone. These two seemingly disconnected devices interacted in ways that were not patently obvious (at least to those who didn't understand radio frequency and electromagnetic interference). Soon, as systems begin to understand the characteristics of every object and how they may relate, such relationships will become more transparent.

There is an axiom in chaos theory that the flap of a butterfly's wings in Australia can cause a storm in Nebraska. The notion is really quite simple: in complex systems, the tiniest of changes can have significant effects at a later state. The challenge with predicting the weather, for example, is those darn butterflies. Certainly, a weather forecaster today has no knowledge of a butterfly on a binge in Sydney—but what if he did? Or, more accurately, what if his machines did? What if they knew every single event that happened, every object that caused it, every location in which events and objects combined—and ran them all through a computer model that found that when a butterfly flapped its wings on the shore near the Sydney Opera House at 3 p.m. on a Tuesday, the likelihood of a thunderstorm forty-eight hours later in Nebraska was 95 percent? Crazy, right? Or is it?

Increasing "Resolution" of Our World

As we've seen in previous chapters, getting better at predicting outcomes in our world means seeing more of its inner workings. And while many people remain skeptical that mere data will provide us with omniscience, I will point to the field of systems biology as an analog. Systems biology is the study of biological organisms at a system-wide level rather than of each part in isolation. It looks at the structure and dynamics of cellular systems, and at how pieces in the system interact.

Looking at the complex interaction between cells and the organism in which they live to figure out why a particular disease manifests requires gathering a massive amount of data—much of it in real time—that "peers into" the human body at the cellular level. Systems biology was seen as an exciting field back in the late 1940s, as researchers begin to think about treating the root cause of disease rather than just the symptoms, but adequate tools to do molecular-level analysis of the human body were hardly in place.

In fact, it was the many advances in molecular biology over the last decades that gave researchers new data, making the in silico model of an organism possible. Once a critical mass of data was available, systems biology became a much more dynamic field.

Suddenly, as with the web, functional genomics emerged in the early '90s, and the human genome itself was mapped in 2001. Functional genomics is all about capturing and understanding interactions among genes and proteins inside our bodies—and this area of study has given us huge amounts of high-quality data about our biological processes. When this new knowledge was coupled with the rise in computing power (the same rise that gave us increasingly realistic gaming devices and special effects in movies, and, frankly, the Internet), our ability to model the biology of humans became possible. In the end, our ability to apply increasingly high-resolution inputs (every year our ability to see inside our bodies, nondestructively and in real time, grows) to massive computing models means we are making dramatic advances in turning what was once an art into a science. In 1997, for example, we were given the first quantitative model of an entire cell, and we are now rushing forth to model entire cellular systems using bioinformatics that describe how our biological systems work, break, and can be repaired.

But what about the softer side of life? To Chomsky's point, gravity means nothing to a computer. And certainly something as complex and difficult to predict as the success of a novel couldn't be computed. Or could it? Recently, at a meeting of the Association of Computational Linguistics, a group presented a paper showing that their system could accurately predict the success of a book (as judged by Pulitzer Prizes, Amazon sales data, and downloads from Project Gutenberg).[2] The software analyzed a book's words, sentence structure, and several other variables in order to make its predictions. Sure, there's no soul there, understanding the beauty of the words or appreciating the elegance of the prose, so maybe Chomsky is right. But it sure feels like we are getting close to, at the least, imbuing a system with a level of understanding that transcends mere computation.

Companies like Beyond Verbal have pioneered systems that use massive amounts of data to analyze your emotions as you talk to them; the programs use human vocal intonations to understand mood, attitudes, and emotional decision making. The iPhone app can provide an on-the-spot emotional diagnosis just by listening to you for twenty seconds. If our systems can recognize emotion, they can likely emulate it. Empathy, after all, is often little more than getting into someone else's headspace.

Machine Learning and Intelligence

Machine learning—an area of AI focusing on systems that "learn" from data in order to navigate future similar scenarios—is one of the ways we've managed to give systems like search the ability to make sense of our analog world. Many of the seemingly magical experiences we have with technology, such as the incredible advances in speech recognition and the more personal interactions we have with retail sites like Amazon, come from this field of study. Machine learning, with its focus on computers' ability to learn without explicit programming, is integral to bridging the gap between humans and search systems.

Think of machine learning in relation to Pandora. When Tim Westergren started the personalized Internet radio service, he employed hundreds of people to listen to music and identify its "features." According to Westergren, the Music Genome Project was an effort to understand music at its most fundamental level by using several hundred attributes that could describe songs.

The group decided to classify music into a number of "genomes": Pop/Rock, Hip-Hop/Electronica, Jazz, World Music, and Classical. Each piece analyzed by one of the companies' genomists would be classified according to nearly four hundred characteristics. They called these characteristics (what we call "features" in search) "genes." In the field of genetics, genes are the sequences of nucleotides that determine whether our eyes are blue, our hair is brown, and whether we tan; they express our inherited makeup. The Music Genome Project focused its energy on classifying what "made up" each song—they were looking for the determining characteristics: Was there a syncopated rhythm? Were there harmonies in the chorus? Did the piece have a string flourish? Were there strong female vocals?

Each song was analyzed by a human and cataloged according to these sorts of traits, with the result that each of the more than three hundred thousand songs in the index had hundreds of descriptions given in granular detail. Moreover, songs weren't catalogued by just one person—the project aimed for constant quality control through analysis by multiple listeners, and the vocabulary and training each genomist received ensured consistency in the musical analysis.

In the case of the Musical Genome Project, humans applied digital attributes to the analog world. They took an analog source—music tracks—and analyzed them to derive "features" of the music. This is what we call "training data," and it is at the heart of a type of machine learning. To understand machine learning, imagine a black box with two sets of data on either side of it. On the left side we have a set of seemingly random data, and on the right side we have what the "sorted" data would look like. So, for example, on the left we might have weather statistics for every day of the past year. On the right, we could have the batting average of every hitter in baseball, by day, over the same year. In supervised machine learning, the system figures out the patterns in a set of data—say, discovering that certain hitters perform better on sunny days (even if they're indoors!). The machine finds a pattern that joins the inputs from the left side of the box and outputs on the right side of the box. It then uses this pattern to make future predictions for similar scenarios.

The process gets even more interesting as you add more features and begin to add weights to the different variables. Imagine that you have information like "average temperatures for June in Seattle" and a fact like "In June, robberies in Seattle are 1.2 times the yearly average." The system is then left to analyze these facts and predict

Machine learning allows systems to see patterns and make predictions.

an outcome. In this case, the system might demonstrate that when temperature rises above sixty-eight degrees in Seattle, robberies are likely to increase. As you add more variables (zip code, time of day), you could begin to build a probabilistic model for when a robbery would occur at your house.

In the case of Pandora, machine learning is used to fine-tune the stations that listeners select. If a person likes a particular song, and Pandora knows all four hundred characteristics of that song, it can predict with some accuracy that the listener will like songs that share those characteristics. When users interact with the system—giving a thumbs-up or thumbs-down to particular songs—the system can further refine its predictions. Maybe a song that Pandora thought I would like but didn't had a higher weighting of the brass instruments gene—knowing that I didn't like that song allows Pandora to rebuild its model for me, and lets that station make predictions for songs that don't have as much brass.

Other examples abound. IBM's Watson, which famously trounced human opponents in the *Jeopardy* game show, has had its capabilities extended to recipe analysis. It turns out that just ten ingredients could yield a trillion or quadrillion possible permutations, especially when you take into account amounts of particular ingredients, like a quarter versus a half teaspoon of red pepper flakes. Watson has now been trained to predict whether a recipe will be pleasant or terrible, surprising or familiar, and it even understands good pairings for particular dishes. This isn't about having a machine with ten thousand recipes in an index, rather it's about Watson having enough training data to begin to understand, much like Pandora does, what will generate a result that meets certain criteria. The complex interplay of factors in a successful recipe is stunning when one stops to think about it. Cooking time, temperature, the interactions of salts and acids: all these elements must be measured and combined in a way that produces a delicious dish. Some have even claimed this new Watson capacity as the first true creativity shown by a machine.

Doing More with Less

One of the most exciting developments in machine learning, however, is that systems are now able to be authoritative with ever *decreasing* amounts of data. This is important, even though we have an explosion of data to mine: collecting, tagging, and using it is still impressively complex. Making accurate predictions and learning more effectively without having to examine all the data is of paramount importance for reasons we will explore in chapter 6. Today, a company called Animetrics can identify a face in a photograph with as few as sixty-five pixels between the eyes. For a standard three-by-five-inch photo, that is about .4 inches. So this system could figure out who you are in a photo where your entire head was the size of your pinkie nail. Further, the company has developed systems that can reconstruct a head shot of a person looking off to the side into a forward-looking shot, which is much simpler and more accurate for facial recognition purposes.[3]

A research study from Stanford recently showed that, with practically no effort, researchers were able to use simple web tools to associate five thousand random phone numbers with people. By adding a little more power, including Google and Intelius, they were able to identify 91 percent of people by name using only phone numbers.

The bottom line? Systems likely won't need the granularity of data required by our friends in systems biology to make the kinds of advances we've talked about in building predictive, intelligent search. While the amount and type of data that systems are gathering continue to expand, the potential for making sense of the world with the data we have available *right now* is both real and growing.

Another Approach:
Mimicking the Human Brain

Beyond the researchers who are exploring machine learning and big sets of data, there are people working to understand how to give our systems more human characteristics and help machines deal with unfamiliar situations. We talked earlier about Ray Kurzweil's research analyzing the brain's workings in great detail in an attempt to figure out how we could build models that mimic the brain in silicon and code. Far from Kurzweil's office on Google's campus, a little group in Bloomington, Indiana, called the Fluid Analogies Research Group, or FARG, is trying a different approach to modeling humanity in systems. As the project lead, Douglas Hofstadter, told the *Atlantic* in 2013, " It was obvious: I don't want to be involved in passing off some fancy program's behavior for intelligence when I know that it has nothing to do with intelligence." In other words, Hofstadter wants to teach computers to think by understanding human intelligence, not simply faking it.

FARG is working on using computers to model *how* we think, not just deploying computing force to make it look like machines are thinking. The beauty of computer systems is that they can be tools to build complex models of our thought processes and, as they are computer code, these processes can be stopped, slowed down, and edited. So we are able, in Hofstadter's view, to tinker with these models to help explain why we think something is funny or why the response from the system seems wacky. If we can analyze each step between hearing and responding, we can pick apart exactly how we ourselves think.

The research Hofstadter is conducting is not performed quickly. Machine learning, as described earlier, can build a model very rapidly; give a system ten billion samples and it will learn the patterns in minutes. Contrast that type of machine learning with Hofstadter's work, where it takes a graduate student five to seven years to turn a relatively simple human thought process into a computer program. As Hofstadter told the *Atlantic*, his work team is like a colony of ants, constantly trying different paths, reporting back to the colony, making errors, and being responsive to new information.

Hofstadter's is not a popular model. The systems built so far are in no way better than humans—in part because they work in very small areas of expertise. And certainly the fathers and grandfathers of artificial intelligence will tell you that, while the work is worthy, it isn't efficient and likely won't produce the same gains as the brute-force computational methods employed today.

But today's work in machine learning offers a glimpse into what's possible. And it certainly echoes Kurzweil's most recent TED Talk, in which he was less concerned about building a system with rules (that fail) and more interested in how the human brain actually understands the world around it. In the end, the beauty of Kurzweil's project to mimic the brain, discussed in chapter 3, is that we might not have to give up humanity for progress.

What About People As a Search Engine?

Beyond more advanced technology, there is an interesting interim step in applying human characteristics to intelligent systems. So far, we have talked about how search can augment our existence by giving us information and helping us with tasks in our lives. But what if it was the other way around? What if people augmented search? Adding humans to the mix can help systems deal with unfamiliar situations and resolve the impedance mismatch.

What if we could fuse human and search capacities to deliver a better overall experience? Edith Law's work on training systems to better handle complex queries is seminal in this space. She looked at what happens when a person queries a search engine about a high-level task such as, "How do I help a family member with ALS?" Today, the engine would return many pages with potentially helpful articles from a variety of sources, but that likely isn't what you, a novice searcher with respect to ALS, would find most helpful. You would want to understand what steps to take to help your family member and in what order, who you might talk to, and how you might best handle the personal affairs of the loved one.

Can we bring the unique talents of humans into the search experience?

What if the system could divide that initial, ambiguous question into pieces and figure out ways to answer each piece? The search system could handle the rote gathering of definitions, names of medical specialists, and lists of drugs, while humans could be asked the softer questions such as, "When can I expect my father to stop being able to eat on his own?" or "How can I help my mother deal with the impact of the disease on my dad?" Then the search engine would recompose the steps or assemble plans to form a coherent response.

Indeed, leveraging individuals' abilities to both solve problems and route information is a key component of the strategy of the team that placed first in the DARPA Network Challenge. The challenge was to find ten moored weather balloons scattered across the United States. You can imagine the near impossibility of ten individuals finding these balloons on their own—indeed, the contest was designed to see how human networks would form to address the challenge. How would one person who saw a red balloon in her backyard alert another person who was looking for it? How would all the reports be reconciled, and how would they be validated? The winning team introduced an incentive mechanism that encouraged individuals to look for balloons and to let their friends know about the task. Rather than rewarding only the person who found the balloon, they rewarded those who invited the person who found the balloon, too. In other words, their system rewarded not just the task completer but the interim people who made it possible.

Slowing Down Search

Part of the work in human-augmented search is an area called slow search, pioneered by Susan Dumais. The question is pretty simple: Why do we expect search to return results in milliseconds? Indeed, quantitative data show that when search time fails to meet certain speed thresholds in standard search, people become markedly less satisfied with the engine. Search engines have trained people to expect instantaneous responses to their questions.

But think about real life. We don't always expect to get a response immediately. Indeed, if people answer a simple question quickly, we ascribe that to honesty (for example, "How old are you?" should generate a near-instant answer). But with more complex questions that aren't easily answered by a "yes" or "no," we often expect a person to pause and think before responding. In fact, if someone answered a complex question too quickly, we might be disquieted or even annoyed, as often the answer is found to be inaccurate. We expect people to take time to consider the question, think through the alternatives, and weigh the best answer before giving a response. Bonus points are awarded if the person asks clarifying questions to make sure his ultimate response actually answers the question. In slow search, Dumais applies that concept to web searching.

Knowing that people who use search expect to get results instantly, and that is how the major search engines have built their interfaces, Dumais and her team asked the question:

What would happen if we gave search engines another two hundred milliseconds to answer a question? What if we gave them two minutes? What about two hours? What would the engines be able to do differently with that amount of time?

It turns out that slow search engenders an entirely new way of thinking about the task and appropriate responses. Rather than "I receive 2.3 words and have to give an answer in forty milliseconds," slow search is, "Now I can do a richer parsing of the items that could resolve the question." The search engine could, much as in Edith Law's work, send off sub-queries to other engines and data stores and wait for their answers. The system could then compile those pieces of data into a more complete answer. For example, if I asked for the best vegetarian restaurant in downtown Seattle, today's search model would immediately return a number of links to pages where some site author consolidated a list of restaurants that had "vegetarian" in their names. But what if search could actually fire off questions to a number of different sources—what if it could ping Yelp, UrbanSpoon, OpenTable, local foodie blogs, CitySearch, Zagat, Frommer's, TripAdvisor, and more? Each of those calls would take up to a second. Then the search system would be blessed with a more complete set of data against which it could apply further analysis (i.e., normalize the rankings, meaning four stars on Yelp equates to 85 percent on UrbanSpoon), run a plotting algorithm to figure out which ones are "downtown," and even reach out to OpenTable to see which ones have tables tonight.

Search might derive a number of characteristics about the restaurants it's finding from all these sources and ask you for clarification, like, "There are a number that appear to be noisy—is that a problem?" or "Do you want to travel more than a couple of miles to get there tonight?" Being able to take a second to have a conversation with the searcher would enable systems to be much more precise in their responses. It would also cater to the human irrationality we prize—the system doesn't need to understand why you want more or less noise, just that you do. By asking, it can fine-tune its responses.

Next, tapping into your social data, search might also look at the other restaurants you've liked on Facebook or checked into on Foursquare and attempt to find a correlation: "If you liked these three restaurants in the past, you are more likely to like such and such restaurant from the list the engine has assembled." A system can do all of this without human intervention, but it would still take several seconds to run the various models against the data.

The challenge today is that people will abandon a search (or keep hitting the search glass in the search bar) when the results don't come back instantly. This is why search engineers have more success when we embed search technologies into things that don't look like search, like Cortana on Windows Phone or Local Scout—both of which do about what I described above but with response times in the seconds. But because it doesn't feel like a keyword search, users are comfortable with that time frame.

Could we take slow search further? Continuing with the example, what if we were to give search thirty minutes to come back with a response? If we gave search an extra thirty minutes we could crowdsource information and ideas. We ask a lot of questions of our social networks, and we don't expect the answers to come back in two hundred milliseconds. We know that if we're willing to wait, we can get better answers. What if search began to post questions on your behalf to your networks? So when I ask search for a good vegetarian restaurant in downtown Seattle, the system could ping a number of my friends who are also vegetarians (or who frequent vegetarian restaurants) and ask them for a recommendation. They might not answer right away—it may take them minutes or even hours—but some fraction of them would likely respond, and when they do, the system could run the same level of computational analysis described above. And the answer is more than formulaic, since my friends know *me* in ways that computer systems, even with the massive amount of data being generated, might not be able to model. People in my networks could give me answers no system could generate; they might know my price sensitivity and the kinds of food I want. For example, I may check in to expensive restaurants quite often—but that might be because I'm on a business trip and someone else is paying for the meal. My friends know I am cheap, so they are likely to answer in ways that are more in sync with my life than a system looking solely at my digital footprints.

This enhanced knowledge about me and my preferences could do more than offer better recommendations. Even the "answers" people see at the top of a search results page for weather and traffic could be improved if engines understood us better. Today, engines don't display more definitive "answers" for more obscure queries because they likely don't have the confidence in the data to place them at the top of the page. Instead, engines give searchers a bunch of links, and the burden is on the searcher to read the pages and figure out the answer.

Dumais and her team have worked on something called "tail answers" in response to queries like, "What's the internal cooking temperature for chicken?" or "How long does it take to roast a turkey per pound?" There are tables on web pages that show the information, but searchers prefer a nice, succinct answer to pages of information they have to slog through. Using slow search, we can break a task down by identifying queries that often lead to the same page on the web. We then get a human worker to highlight an answer in that page, have someone else create a little snippet, have somebody proofread it, and get someone to send it back to the user. In a few minutes we can do something like that today, but it doesn't really feel like search. These results would look like artificial intelligence to a searcher who doesn't know the behind-the-scenes mechanism, but really they are more like the product of augmented intelligence, with humans supplying the augmentation.

Thinking about how humans could play a role in search also gives us insights into how nonhuman augmented search systems could develop. For example, according to researcher Eric Horvitz, it takes six months to a year for current medical research to be published. And even once it's published, it can take as long as a decade for doctors across the world to become aware of and internalize the research. That's up to ten years before new research makes it to the level of a medical practice, in some instances.

Now, if a search system had access to all this diagnostic information, a diagnosis might take about thirty minutes; search results could give the patient or doctor the probability of the different things that could be happening medically. The system would give reasons for its diagnosis based on the data it had; for example, results might note that a particular piece of research text highlights a high probability that, if the patient has a brown-colored spot and a feeling of numbness, it is due to this particular condition. The system is generating a hypothesis and showing its reasoning. So now we as a society have a ten-year gap in the relay of medical information being condensed to fifteen or thirty minutes, and it will all happen while a patient is at the doctor's office, thanks to search technologies.

Can Humans Compensate for Errors in "Small Data"?

Despite what we saw in earlier chapters about burgeoning data, our data stores are still relatively sparse. It's true that billions of devices are contributing to a model of the real world housed on the web, and yes, more signals are created every day by our online tasks. But search is still very, very far away from being able to know that butterfly in Sydney flapped its wings. Our collective ability to predict the future enters into the realm of what scientists call the bias-variance tradeoff: as systems attempt to define at a more granular level what the searcher might like and do, the amount of data they have to work with is diminished. Why? Simply because there isn't as much data on an individual as there is on a group of us. So the more systems attempt to make predictions using smaller and smaller segments of data, the less accurate the statistics get and the more errors they will make.

There are a number of examples in science where small sample sizes generated silly predictions. One famous example involves Sir Richard Peto, who was required to subsegment a study looking at the effect of aspirin as an acute treatment for heart attacks. As Peto explains, "The study proceeded with a controlled randomization of approximately 17,000 heart attack patients. There were 1,000 deaths in the placebo arm compared to 800 deaths in the aspirin-treated arm. That equates to a five standard error difference in mortality, which is an excellent result."

That is a material difference but the academic publication refused to publish the results unless Peto's team showed which "subsegments" (old, young, black, white, male, female) would benefit most from the study. Knowing that they had too little data to make meaningful predictions about that—and thus that they were likely to generate false negatives—the team told the publication "no." The publication insisted, and so the team decided to subsegment by astrological sign. And indeed, their analysis showed that aspirin didn't work as a treatment for Libras or Geminis, but worked well if you were a Capricorn. Indeed, as Peto said, "It's just complete junk. And actually, a lot of subgroup analyses are just junk."

All this is to say that until we have the ability to figure out when the butterfly flaps its wings in Australia, and get enough data to avoid the bias-variance tradeoff, using humans to help the search process along makes sense, as we are able to rationalize our way through sparse sets of data in a way machines are not.

Fast, Slow, but Coming

If we step back and reflect on what we've explored so far, it appears that this next phase of search as a hinge is not only possible, it is likely inevitable. Even if we don't reach the level of the *Star Trek* computer in the next five years, many interim steps—such as incorporating people into search and building systems that are expert in particular domains—will edge us toward a future that verges on magic. Even if we can't agree on how soon that future will arrive, there is little doubt about one thing: tomorrow's web—and therefore search—will look different from today's.

CHAPTER 5

What Search Will Bring Us

The idea that I can talk to my Martian-branded Watch—say, ask it a question about a football player—and have it relay all the information I want back to me in an easy-to-understand voice is as old as science fiction, yet the ability to do that seems trivial today. Search, in my opinion, offers us superpowers the potential of which we are just barely able to comprehend.

As we've seen, search can be and do so much more than answer trivial questions. Machine and device-level intelligence will eventually stitch together data about everything in the world in a way that clarifies for us the action we should take in a given situation.

Today's systems are isolated, but tomorrow's search will allow systems to connect with one another and optimize our world. Right now, your air conditioning system can't talk to your window shades and tell them to lower to reduce your electricity bill. Your car doesn't talk to traffic lights to reroute you around one that isn't functioning. Besides the fact that these systems currently don't have any way to connect to one another, even if they *could* talk to other devices they wouldn't make any sense because they don't speak the same language.

Search systems can and will power machine-level intelligence so that, in the future, your air conditioner will notice it is getting hot in your apartment, will query search to understand why it is getting hot and realize it's because sunlight is coming in your windows, and will ask search how it can stop sunlight from coming in. Finally, because search tells it that moving an opaque cover over a window will reflect solar energy, and because search knows blinds are opaque covers, your air conditioner can tell the blinds to close until the temperature drops. Systems will be able to understand the real world and take action on your behalf.

Assuming we have the systems, the question becomes, how do we imbue ourselves with superpowers and use them effectively? We must fundamentally rethink what search is, how people use it, and what we should demand of it. Today's search gives us what we want, not what we deserve. The following chapter explores some of those potentials as we traverse the chasm from where we are today to where we aspire to be.

Search Will Augment Reality

When search systems are part of the world, not just observers of it, our surroundings will "light up" with information about everything around us. Technology start-up Estimote is working to combine sensors in ways that provide digitally inspired intelligence in the real world. Small beacons placed throughout retail establishments use low-power Bluetooth to interact with customers' mobile devices.

These beacons serve two purposes: first, they allow businesses to push location-based personal alerts to customers. For example, as you pass by a pair of shoes, you might get an alert that they are on sale—in the future, as these devices are linked into search intelligence that understands both the world and your preferences in great detail, the alerts will have the capacity to advise you that the shoes will go well with the pants you purchased last week. Beyond that, these sensors are able to track how long customers gaze at certain items on a shelf, how long they spend in certain aisles, and the patterns they follow in the store. This is one of the most fascinating examples of blending cheap, real-world sensors (which, as we discussed in chapter 1, are now possible) with the ubiquitous smartphones to deliver an augmented physical experience that doesn't require the user to change his habits. The goal is to build Amazon-like experiences for brick-and-mortar retailers by allowing customers to find items more efficiently, but more importantly letting systems recommend other products or deals you might enjoy based on your interests or past purchases, a scenario we take for granted when shopping online.

> Search will "light up" the reality around us with web-derived intelligence.

The fusion of hardware and these next-generation search systems also offer unprecedented advances in understanding humanity, both our behavior and our motivations. For example, Microsoft's Xbox One console lets you control your television using your voice and gestures, and the Kinect sensor that makes that possible also has some unique features. Because of its cutting-edge hardware, Kinect can do things like monitor heart rate from across the room, no contact required. It can see your posture, emotions on your face, where you're looking, and much more. In essence, it's easy to imagine a future in which you ask your Kinect to find you something to watch on a Friday night and, rather than relying on you tagging movies you like in a Netflix queue, the Kinect system selects from a model it has built based on the movies you've watched that caused an emotional response. Building a model that interprets changes in heart rate, how often you laugh or cry, and if you are paying attention over the course of the programs you watched will give Kinect a far better idea of what you *really* like. I may say I like *Wings of the Dove,* and that may be what I tell everyone. But when I'm alone on a Friday, Kinect may know that I am really in the mood for *Con Air* because the system has noticed how much I enjoy action movies on Fridays.

Fully and partially augmented experiences using devices like Oculus Rift and Google Glass also point the way forward. There are many books written about this topic, including *Age of Context* by Robert Scoble and Shel Israel, but the implication for search in particular is profound. How? The ability for a person to simply gaze at an object and have the system tell her what she is looking at isn't only technologically possible, it's in full production with an app called FieldTrippr on Google Glass. The app launches when the wearer of Glass says "Okay, Glass, explore nearby," and it highlights nearby attractions and restaurants along with details about the wearer's location from more than one hundred publishers about the architecture of the city, historical events, and insider tips.

As companies develop better lenses on the world—whether they are positioned over our eyes or elsewhere on our bodies—search systems will supplement our natural existence by telling us things we wouldn't otherwise know, and they'll do this organically, without us asking.

Finally, systems like Microsoft Research's Project Louise enable you to direct systems to supplement your real-world conversations with "just-in-time information." Imagine you are having a conversation in Skype and, as you're talking, the system (with both people's permission) is listening in the background. When you tell your coworker in Beijing that you are taking him to a great dinner on Friday when he arrives, the system passively detects your intent and, in real time, finds a restaurant and presents it to you as you are talking. In this sense, search literally augments your real-world, natural human interactions in a way that lets both parties have access to information and services as they go about their normal day.

In Focus: Zemanta

Zemanta, a content and links suggestion plugin, is currently deployed across millions of blogs. The system watches what an author is writing and augments it with real-world knowledge. If you are writing an article about the Bay of Pigs Invasion, for example, Zemanta recognizes that you are discussing a historical event and asks if you would like to augment that phrase with inline knowledge for your readers. As you write papers or posts, the system works to understand and supplement your own knowledge with information from the wider world. Zemanta is only one example, but it offers a glimpse at the powerful implications of search as a set of senses and abilities that can be employed rather than as a simple blank box to be filled with keywords.

Search Will Augment Our Natural Abilities

Imagine being able to offload from your brain information and tasks that can be better handled by a search system. As we discussed in chapter 3, this new model of search, which lets us outsource analysis of the trillions of pieces of data around us, could radically increase our productivity and happiness. Just as our smartphones have freed our brains from having to remember phone numbers, the new generation of search platforms will allow us to selectively and quietly offload items that today demand our attention.

Think how liberating it would be to not only never forget anything, but to not have to think about the fact that you are never forgetting anything. One interesting project was described to me by Susan Dumais, distinguished scientist at Microsoft Research: the idea is that if a system can understand everything you've ever seen and for how long you've seen it, it can make some assumptions about how likely you are to have forgotten that thing. How is this possible? In the old days (ten years ago), an "eye tracker" could be purchased for $40,000, and it would examine where a person was looking on a screen. In search, we used eye trackers extensively to understand the areas of a web page people paid attention to. Today these devices can be had for as little as $200, and the built-in webcams on every computer, tablet, and phone are rapidly becoming good enough to enable eye tracking without special hardware.

Imagine never forgetting anything—or more appropriately—never having to remember.

Why is this eye-tracking ability important and how will it be used? Imagine you are looking at a news page or a set of search results. Today, every time you visit that page, even if it's one you frequent often, you have to identify what is new since you last visited. In other words, even if you have seen the navigation link bar on the NBC news page a thousand times, on the one thousand and first time you'll expend a fraction of cognitive load seeing if anything has changed. As humans, we have learned to tune out those parts that have likely not changed—but what if they have? With eye tracking, the system understands what you look at each time you come to the page. And each time you come back, it can highlight what changed for you.

In another application, a system would know what you have read in an article and would simply pick up where you left off rather than you having to remember and find again the last thing you read. And finally, there are profound impacts for learning. Using a combination of eye tracking and semantic understanding, a system could dynamically adapt to teach you things you likely do not know. Today, even if you already know

90 percent of the material covered in an article on the U.S. electoral process, *you* have to find the 10 percent you don't know. That means you need to read through the whole article, when all you really needed to see is the piece that contributes the highest marginal return on your effort. Systems that adapt learning to what you likely don't know can and will be built.

Systems that use eye tracking can also remind users more effectively than their own biological memory. Primary research has shown how probabilistic models can predict which items you have seen but may have forgotten, how relevant those items might be in a given situation, and the cost to your attention if the system interrupts you with a reminder.[1]

Dr. Eric Horvitz, whom we met earlier, has built a system called Lifebrowser that navigates vast stores of personal information. He's kept nearly twenty years of his personal and work communications, documents, photos, and videos, and lets Lifebrowser index it. I will never forget the first time I saw it, back in 2007 or so—he put my name into the system and it pulled up, in a microsecond, an e-mail I had sent him in 1998. Even more compelling, though, is Lifebrowser's ability to augment Horvitz's memory of that communication with a photo of a wedding he was attending at around the same time. So it's not just a search, which today is relatively easy for cloud-based e-mail systems, but the comingling of all of a person's private data, so that memory is jogged to more fully recollect the interaction. We still don't understand how the brain or memory works, but we do know that subtle stimuli can cause latent memories to bubble to the surface.

Lifebrowser works by using machine-learning techniques to derive what is "important" to the user. *MIT Tech Review* offers a nice explanation:

When judging photos, Lifebrowser looks at properties of an image file for clues, including whether the file name was modified or the flash had fired. It even examines the contents of a photo using machine-vision algorithms to learn how many people were captured in the image and whether it was taken inside or outdoors. The "session" of photos taken at one time is also considered as a group, for cues such as how long an event was and how frequently photos were taken.[2]

The system orchestrates not retrieval of dates, people, or topics, but also the "landmarks" the system thinks are necessary for one to fully recollect the situation. Augment this power with systems that can alert and supplement your real-world interactions with people, places, and things, and you can begin to see how the more capable web combined with personal data stores can unlock massive potential. This ability to balance multitasking (something we're actually not very good at as a species) with attention (when should the system break in?) and memory (are you likely to have forgotten this?) has the potential to extend our natural abilities in a very personalized way.

In Focus: Knowing the Future

Marc Davis, the scientist who has pioneered many human computer interaction models, painted an interesting picture of how search can be used not just to retrieve information or match intent to a service, but also to predict and augment *future intents*. It's the ability to, for example, understand that I have arrived at a location and know the likely next things that I will do based on my patterns and on what search knows about me.

> Search isn't about just finding things in the past; it's about predicting what should happen.

According to Davis:

> Imagine a typical meeting scenario. I wanted to read through the e-mail that the organizer sent in advance but that wasn't in the actual appointment on my phone. Now, at home I can just search and find the mail, but say I was on a bike, so that wasn't possible.
>
> What a truly intelligent system should have done was, as I was biking from my physical therapist to home to get ready for our meeting, the e-mail should have been read to me on my headset on my phone because it knew right then I had enough time to absorb this information by listening in advance of the meeting.

Apps like Refresh and Humin approximate this service today. The system says, *"Here's who you're meeting with today. Here's information on each person."* Currently, the system only profiles people but what if it knew more than that? What if it knew the content I was planning to discuss and how I should prep beforehand? And what if it could alert me to the points I should bring up when I get to the meeting based on who is attending and what we last talked about in e-mail? Suddenly, we leave search behind as merely an information retrieval system and see the benefits of having an agent augment what I am likely to *want* to know.

Search Will Allow for Real-Time Decision Making

Imagine tapping into the collective knowledge of the world in real time to make better decisions. More interestingly, think about how news was reported even a few years ago: a news bureau found out about the event; a reporter was assigned to gather facts, write about it, and publish it the next day on paper, within a few hours on TV, or, finally, within an hour on a website. Clearly, the time taken from incident to reporting could affect your ability to make a better decision that could radically affect your happiness. With the advent of real-time and social updates—and the processing power we now have to make sense of them—the time between incident and decision can be shrunk to minutes. Anirudh Koul, researcher at Microsoft Research and formerly at Yahoo, gives a great example regarding the shooting at Los Angeles International Airport in 2013:

> The LAX shooting happened on a regular day, but when the shooting happened, people started tweeting about it. Their friends saw it, they retweeted or added color like, "Hope everybody is safe." In about ten or fifteen minutes, the press started getting phone calls and they started to write in their own Twitter feeds. By about the twentieth minute, the first articles about it started to appear.
>
> Now, there's a gap of this twenty minutes from incident to first article. From that point onward, for other news publications to catch up, it took another ten minutes. So it wasn't until the thirtieth minute that other stories began to break. The television media also started to come up in the thirty-fifth minute. You can easily see that there's a big gap, even for a breaking news story, from what happened to when it really became a trend in media.

Koul asks us to imagine instead using the massive numbers of signals available in real time and social media. "Using those feeds as a signal, we could detect something anomalous in the first ten minutes," he says, meaning we could flag the event for people somewhere between ten and twenty minutes earlier than they otherwise would have known—and that's if they were paying attention to their favorite news sites. "Imagine if you're right there in the airport itself or you're going to the airport, if you got an alert saying, something has happened there and it's still not reported in the news but we think there is something to this, that would be a really, really good user scenario."

You're already seeing versions of this power in particular domains. Waze, for example, uses the power of people's mobile phones to monitor speeds on streets and highways and aggregate that data to provide real-time decision making regarding directions from one place to another. It even allows for reporting by drivers of police, speed cameras, or other incidents on the road that gets passed to other users of the platform.

Where it *does* get problematic is in the more general application of the technology. For example, why would a particular system be looking for events at LAX at the time of the shooting? They wouldn't. But by relying on trends and spikes, which can be compared to the norm for that entity, systems could identify that something out of the ordinary is happening and could dispatch other machines to look more closely across the other data streams to which they have access.

A Superhuman Humanity

I hope you will agree that the coming age of search has the potential to bring promising advancements in both work and play. I, for one, am excited for the day when Dr. Horvitz's memory augmentation helps me recall effortlessly something I need to ask a person when I see him next. Or the time when Dr. Dumais's cheap eye-tracking technology helps me read the article I started on the train seamlessly by marking my place as I move from device to device. Or when I am able to discover more information about something merely by look-ing at it. Having the collective intelligence and wisdom of the world—the true promise of the Internet—at my beck and call seems almost too good to be true.

And to an extent, it is.

We didn't end up with today's search because of apathy on the part of the companies that develop it. There are genu-ine technical, personal, and societal challenges that keep this vision of search at bay. So what's holding us back?

CHAPTER 6

What Holds Search Back: The Technology

The digital utopia that the next generation of search promises to usher in is in no way a done deal. Many obstacles stand in the path of progress toward this high level of search omniscience. However, a look at each obstacle yields many ideas for entirely new companies, academic ventures, and research projects that could generate not just a profoundly different society, but the next locus of wealth in the world. This chapter is the first of two that highlight the challenges facing this new world of search superpowers; first we'll look at the technical hurdles and in the second half, the business and societal realities inherent in moving from the known world toward the future to which we should aspire.

The Islands

One of the major challenges hampering the development of a helpful, predictive hinge that lets humanity think at the speed of computers while maintaining the things that make us human is the access to and ownership of data. As we've discussed, the amount of data being generated by people, devices, and services is growing at an astounding rate. But just because the data exists doesn't mean we all have equal access to it—nor should we.

Think of the data Amazon has about your purchasing habits. Or the information Facebook has about your connections and likes. Or what the IRS knows about your deductions and the charities you give money to every year. Or the data your credit card companies have about where you spend your money. In each case, the data is "owned" by the company. One could make the case that the data is actually owned by the person who created it (i.e., you), but because we use many of these services for free, we in essence sign away our sole-ownership rights of this data. We'll talk more about that in the next chapter. Putting aside the ownership discussion for now, the fact is that these companies and agencies collect and store significant amounts of data about us—and it isn't shared freely.

This is the case for at least a couple of reasons: companies want to maintain a competitive advantage by making use of the data for their own ends and consumers often don't want their information shared without their consent. The result of these restrictions, however, is that we cannot achieve a truly open and powerful form of search. From a consumer perspective, it means you constantly have to tell services your preferences and identifying information (zip code, interests, phone number, etc.). It also means services can't be tailored to your needs more effectively. It is highly inconvenient that my purchase history from Amazon (and the fact that I tend to buy a lot of electronics) isn't carried over to Kickstarter, where that data could be used to recommend interesting projects I might wish to fund, or that my purchases on iTunes aren't used to trigger notifications to me from StubHub when a band whose songs I consistently buy is coming to town.

From a company perspective, consider the amount of

When companies have only pieces of your data profile, the effectiveness of search is curtailed.

money spent to buy data from third-party data brokers (like Experian or Intelius) so the business can get a more complete picture of its customers. How much customer loyalty is squandered because of small companies' inability to tap into the vast data resources available to these larger companies, data that would allow these small companies to offer customers things that might make their lives better? The short-term gain many companies achieve by keeping this data to themselves is likely dwarfed by the value they could attain if they shared data, or at least had access to the data consumers wanted them to have.

Imagine if you, the consumer and user, owned all your data and housed it in a single place, allowing your interactions with dozens of different online and offline companies to feed into a personal profile that you control. We'll discuss some of the work done in this area in the next chapter, and the potential is amazing.

A Profile of You

There have been some efforts to create a single digital profile: Facebook Login, for example, offers application developers the ability to tap into the vast resources contained in many people's Facebook profiles. This is a great step in that we as consumers can reuse some of the hard-earned profile data we've spent time curating on Facebook. But alas, the applications or sites that use Facebook as their login mechanism can't really augment that single profile. In other words, if you book a taxi with the Taxi Magic app, the fact that you always book it from the same location doesn't get communicated to Facebook. You still, in essence, create an island of information in the taxi app, which is typically not useable by any other application.

There are plenty of good reasons companies don't want to share data about their customers. Stringent privacy laws in both U.S. states and countries outside the United States impose heavy penalties on companies that let their users' information escape out into the ether. And no company wants to be the one that allows a bad actor to glean information about a customer that is used to perpetuate a crime in either the physical or digital world.

Ideally, we need a broker for the islands of data. Search systems could be used to do much of the brokering—by having access to all your different personas, search could function as the honest broker that doesn't store information from these various islands, but facilitates access as needed to complete a task. Imagine you're in Macy's and you'd like to find a pair of shoes to complement an outfit you bought on Nordstrom. com last week. Search could handle that request—but you'd need to give it permission to do so. So when you ask, as you are standing in Macy's, "What shoes would look good with the suit I bought last week?" search would have to understand that you have accounts at many stores (Amazon, Bluefly, Nordstrom) and would need to prompt you for permission to talk to those stores' web services to figure out what you bought last week before it could conduct the computation required to advise you of the shoes in Macy's inventory that might complement your recent purchase.

None of this is technologically impossible: websites could offer standard methods to call into customer data; authentication mechanisms used by your trusted search service could talk to the sites; and companies that have spent time and money to curate your data could still make use of it for their own proprietary goals. But the incentive for any company or agency to do so at this point in time seems fuzzy. There is certainly an entirely new industry to be born that could enable, with customer permission, data to be shared across heterogeneous profiles maintained by the players in the space. Industry-standard protocols like bounties, or paying people for their customer referrals, could be a model for this collaboration. However, there needs to be a system in place where everyone—including the consumer—benefits from the data sharing.

Hardware As an Island

Another potential dark force in the future of search is companies' increasing practice of using hardware to build moats for their services, meaning that, through their choice of a device or object, people place most of their data in a closed system. I predict that a company or entrepreneur will soon create a license-free hardware platform, complete with basic wireless networking, and will offer hardware, software, support, and a services stack behind it. They will offer this hardware solution very cheaply or even for free for those builders that commit to using the company's backend to host the services the device requires and that promise to integrate to the company's larger search, subscription, and advertising platform. While this may sound great, this move will likely encourage another silo of user data, preventing our ultimate search dream from coming true.

(In)Security

If there is one thing that keeps me up at night in this increasingly connected and interdependent world of devices, it is the difficult problem of security. In popular culture, we saw the fatal attack on the vice president's pacemaker in Showtime's *Homeland* series[1] (and, according to at least some hackers, the only implausible note was the distance of the attacker from the vice president; other than that, the deed is apparently doable).

In real life, a hacker took control of a baby monitor that was connected to the Internet and was able to make lewd comments to the baby, move the camera to get a better view of the room, and even speak to the parents when they entered the room after hearing a strange voice.[2]

And there is no end of stories about remote exploitation of people's webcams, whereby attackers have even figured out how to activate the camera without turning on the telltale light (ever wonder why people put electrical tape over their laptop's camera?). But this is a bit different from the other two, in that exploiting unpatched computers is as old as computers themselves. The real advance—if one can call it that—is that now bad actors are working to take control of the billions of sensors and devices all around us. And, unlike computer operating systems, these devices often don't have an upgrade function or even a company that is patching devices against the exploitation.

The problem of devices as a new method of attack was described brilliantly by security expert Bruce Schneier in early 2014.[3] He highlighted the fact that all these little devices we carry or install in our homes and cars are often made up of tiny chips that need to be cheap in order to keep the end-unit cost down. Because the chips are so cheap and profit margins are very slim, the companies that make them do as little engineering as possible while still trying to differentiate their products with added features. The devices that connect us to the web and to each other also threaten us. The assemblers of devices often opt for price and availability, and even the companies with their names on the devices often don't add more than a user interface on top of this hodgepodge of chips and silicon.

The challenge, then, is security on these "Frankendevices," when no company is ultimately accountable or has an incentive to do the sorts of engineering and updates that software companies have been doing for a decade. Even when the chips that power the devices are of a new design, the software that runs on top of them and powers our routers, smart switches, and an increasing number of devices may be ancient. As Schneier says in his blog:

>...the software is old, even when the device is new. For example, one survey of common home routers found that the software components were four to five years older than the device. The minimum age of the Linux operating system was four years. The minimum age of the Samba file system software: six years. They may have had all the security patches applied, but most likely not. No one has that job. Some of the components are so old that they're no longer being patched. This patching is especially important because security vulnerabilities are found "more easily" as systems age.[4]

Even if we are careful with our gear—I can almost see an industry of bespoke electronics that can trace their lineage and have dedicated engineering teams making sure they are secure—the things we put *into* our gear, like memory cards or USB devices, may put us at risk. One of the most interesting examples of this, which has come to light recently, is that MicroSD cards (or any sort of flash memory), which we use in our computers, cameras, video cameras, and anything else where we need extra gigabytes of storage, can be turned into Trojans against us.[5] Again, because price is one of the major determiners for both manufacturers and consumers, flash RAM is often sourced from many partners and the manufacturers expect significant numbers of defects in the storage. True error-free storage is expensive to manufacture at scale, so manufacturers rely instead on microcomputers in these chips to handle the errors that inexpensive storage generates.

Andrew Huang, a security researcher, notes: "In modern implementations, the microcontroller will approach 100 MHz performance levels, and also have several hardware accelerators on-die. Amazingly, the cost of adding these controllers to the device is probably on the order of $0.15 to $0.30." Keep in mind, 100 MHz was about the speed of a $3,500 computer in the late 1990s, capable of running Windows 98 on up.

Worse, these microcomputers are explicitly designed for easy updating by the manufacturer to account for the specific algorithms required to correct the bad sectors in memory. Which means that, for a researcher at a recent DEF CON Hacking Conference, it was easy to break into one of these microcomputers and upload a small computer program that the device would dutifully execute. Such exploits enable a nearly undetectable "man-in-the-middle" scenario in which everything going to and from that device could be open to an attacker.

There are no easy solutions here, and the threats are very real. The industry, in order to engender trust in users, will have to take steps to provide as many redundant safeguards as possible both on devices and on the systems that monitor them for us.

Drowning in Data

Contrary to popular belief, just because data exists doesn't mean search systems can do anything with it. Bing receives three billion updates a day from Facebook (a fraction of the five billion or so per day generated by Facebook at the end of 2013), and each update is rife with information (time, place, people, links, comments, etc.).

This year, humans will create 100 billion 32GB iPads' worth of data.

If you think about the numbers, it's easy to lose your ability to comprehend both the scale and possible purpose of the data.

In 2014, humans will create more than three zettabytes of information—that's the equivalent of 100 billion 32GB iPads. If you stacked that many iPads, they would equal the volume of nearly four Great Walls of China. Another comparison: three zettabytes is equivalent to every person in the U.S. tweeting three tweets per minute for more than thirty-eight thousand years. Again, this is the amount of data we will create *this year.* Even more spectacularly, in 2015, the number will double.

It may seem like we're whipsawing around: on the one hand, computing power is nearly infinite and on the other, we have too much data to process. And while it is never a good idea to bet against the inexorable advances in computing capacity and speed, a story about IBM's famous Watson computer, the one that beat human players on *Jeopardy* in 2012, is telling. When the IBM engineers were building Watson years ago, according to data scientist Anirudh Koul, the system would take almost an hour to answer a particular question. *Almost an hour.*

They worked for three years to improve that time through better algorithms and parallelizing the systems, and got it to the point where it took around 2.5 seconds on average to answer a question. And what powered Watson? Ninety servers, comprised of 2,880 processors and 16TB of RAM in which all its knowledge was stored. It weighed eighteen tons and required ten refrigerators worth of cooling equipment, generating forty tons of cooling capacity. It wasn't even connected to the Internet. And it could handle precisely one question at a time in 2008.

> IBM's Watson needed ten refrigerators to keep it cool enough to answer one question at a time.

Koul says, "Now imagine a modern search system—it handles *tens of thousands* of queries per second. Considering it was taking Watson 2.5 seconds to answer each question—and that was with one at a time—you can imagine how this wouldn't scale to a modern search experience."

At a certain point, we begin to brush up against the laws of physics. If a system has to traverse nine different informational graphs and analyze one hundred web pages, as well as derive the dominant entity in the page and apply a natural language filter on top to extract all those things that a searcher is looking for, we are almost to the point where just the number of calls both within a system and across remote systems means we're getting into twenty to thirty milliseconds just to handle the overhead before any real computation is done!

This is why companies are building their own knowledge graphs—just like Watson had 16TB of the web stored in its memory—so they can reduce the number of other machines, and networks, that these intelligent systems will have to talk to. But there is no guarantee that this will be enough to outstrip the production of data.

Tricks of the Trade

Anirudh Koul again gives us insight into some ways to deal with the mass of data and combat the issue of data outpacing our ability to process it. He relays an example of one of the most exciting applications—energy management in the home (well, it's exciting to me). To understand how massive big data can get, imagine every outlet in your house talking to a "smart meter." In the era of big data, one would be tempted to collect every measurement possible. That means, since our power operates at 60 Hz, you could get a reading sixty times a second. Multiply that by 3,600 seconds in an hour, and then multiply that by every outlet in your house. You can see the staggering amount of data you would create in just one hour.

And capturing all that data is what we traditionally would have done, because we could never be sure what was going to be useful. Given the explosion of data in the last two years, that model seems to be falling out of favor. Koul recalls the time five years ago when he was working at Carnegie Mellon University and was trying to process just 1 percent of the real-time Twitter feed, which resulted in his computer burning up two processors in a year and multiple hard drive failures.

Koul says, of data and home energy management:

> I had worked on a machine learning problem where, based on the smart meter data that you could get, we could actually predict when you started the toaster oven, or you started your washing machine without actually ever asking what you started or what you didn't. This knowledge was based on spikes in electricity consumption and how the frequency of electricity changes when you start a particular electric-powered device in your home. The electric company wanted to know this data because then they could really know how to model the rates for peak electricity, how to better generate and serve, and how not to produce electricity that would just go to waste. To find those kinds of patterns initially they would start just recording everything.

You can see the problem here; the electric company had specific questions about usage, and while it's tempting to think it could find all these answers if it had every microsecond of data, the company quickly realized the daunting nature of the task. It also didn't make sense to track everything if all you were looking for was a change in state (a spike or a different frequency on the line); there was no point in keeping data that was several cycles removed from the state change.

Koul realized that, instead of recording all those individual hertz-seconds of data, he should look at the data in increments of minutes. At that level of detail, he could see that an appliance was started or stopped at a particular time. After a day or two, he just deleted the previous data, which was not worth keeping. "So literally, even though we probably can mechanically store all this data—we have the disk space to do it—figuring out what you want to do with it all post-hoc is very, very computationally expensive," Koul says.

Using this aggregation method, Koul was able to achieve the utility company's goal without unnecessarily mining trillions of bits of relatively useless data. He was still able to see the patterns the data were exposing, but he did it by isolating the interesting moments in time, building a model of those moments, and discarding the other noisy data once the model was complete.

But his example demonstrates more than just clever techniques for data mining. It also points to the fact that we need to do some serious thinking about the information we're creating. Koul argues that we should go into this new world of search thinking about what we want to accomplish, and should collect data to support those goals. Rather than gathering all the data that's possible—with the concomitant risks and complexity—we should collect only what we need to achieve the outcomes we desire. Now, I'm fully aware that this may sound as silly as the skeptic who once said, "Who will need more than 640KB on their computer?" It's easy to get caught up in the limitations of today and design future states that reflect current reality. We may very well achieve a breakthrough in quantum computing that makes the consternation around data processing moot. But then we must ask ourselves if we even want all that data. There are certainly those who make the case that that amount of data is a danger to individual freedoms, so why bother keeping it all?

Big Data: Does Size Matter?

Despite what I've written in previous chapters, we should not delude ourselves into thinking that data is a panacea that will enable us to predict the future with certainty and assist us with 100 percent fidelity. A professor at NYU and a principal researcher at Microsoft Research, danah boyd is one of the preeminent thinkers on digital selves, social networks, and big data. She rightly highlights in her 2011 paper the perils of trying to see everything as eminently quantifiable:

> Spectacular errors can emerge when researchers try to build social science findings into technological systems. A classic example arose when Friendster chose to implement Robin Dunbar's (1998) work. Analyzing gossip practices in humans and grooming habits in monkeys, Dunbar found that people could only actively maintain 150 relationships at any time and argued that this number represented the maximum size of a person's personal network. Unfortunately, Friendster believed that people were replicating their pre-existing personal networks on the site, so they inferred that no one should have a friend list greater than 150. Thus, they capped the number of "Friends" people could have on the system.[6]

We all know how Friendster turned out. As boyd points out, just because data is big, it isn't necessarily complete. True statistical representations need to come from controlled (either random or otherwise) samples. Big data, culled from the billions of people and sensors now speaking on the Internet, is full of gaps, discontinuities, and blatantly inaccurate data. And, as boyd notes, these errors can easily compound as we join our graphs together.

Big data isn't always complete data.

Careful researchers are always concerned about biases in their data. They model their hypotheses and experiments after the limitations of their data sets. When presented with lossy, sparse, or even just temporal data from the noisy contributors to the Internet, where they can't possibly know the provenance of the information, researchers may draw suspect conclusions from the data. To make this idea concrete, imagine for a moment that some system collects all your browsing data from your PC for a day. It notes that you favor sites about Italian vacations. If that is all the data it has, the conclusion it may draw about you (that you like Italy) may not be valid. By ignoring the history from other devices and your browsing history on other days, the system could mis-profile you in an epic way.

Finally, boyd says big data "...encourages the practice of apophenia: seeing patterns where none actually exist, simply because massive quantities of data can offer connections that radiate in all directions." This harkens back to the old adage about "lies, damn lies, and statistics," whereby you can use numbers to make many things seem true that actually aren't.

Big Data and Unintended Outcomes

Our ability to capture, analyze, and predict outcomes based on the ever-increasing fidelity of the digital world means we do not have to be victims of unseen forces but can instead be active participants in influencing our future. We must be careful with this power and balance our ability to predict against the accuracy of our predictions. After all, if we predict that traffic will be horrible on the bridge tonight because there is a basketball game at the downtown arena, we could potentially cause other negative effects, like shifting traffic to side streets that are not set up to handle the increased load. Worse still is not knowing if we made the right decision—what if fewer people attended the game because it was, say, too cold? Then our model would be inaccurate, and we could have influenced reality for the worse.

It reminds me of the time travel paradox in *Back to the Future*, where Marty McFly was told in no uncertain terms by Doc not to tamper with the past. Why? Because outcomes in the future are unpredictable. Even meeting his soon-to-be mom in a café increased the possibility that he would never be born, if she had fallen in love with him rather than his father. To relate this to our current scenario, imagine if we predicted you would get stomach cancer because, through our genetic and environmental prediction models, we linked a diet heavy in red meat to a high likelihood of contracting the disease. So you switch to a diet of all fish and plants. Let's say that at this point in the future all fish are genetically modified because of our dilapidated natural stocks, so you end up consuming hundreds of pounds of fish over ten years and contract some other disease related to the GMO product. In this situation, the system used available data to steer you away from one calculated risk but ended up pointing you in a direction where the outcome was as bad or worse. And the path the system pointed you down was wrong *and no one even knew it* because it wasn't until some time into the decade of fish consumption that we realized this particular genetic modification to fish caused human disease.

Here is where the examples diverge. In *Back to the Future*, where Marty knew the future, perfect data could make sure he steered clear of his mother in 1950s California and never interacted with people or events that could have orbital overlap with his mother. In our fish example, however, we can only make assumptions about the relative risks of future outcomes. Because there wasn't enough data to understand that GMO fish was toxic (it was newly introduced and therefore no "training data," as discussed in chapter 4, existed), the system actually made a bad decision for the person concerned. The good news, of course, is that future system-level actions would benefit from this knowledge, so other likely stomach cancer patients would be steered clear of eating this fish; but for the initial prediction, the guess was wrong.

> Perfect data doesn't exist; we must deal with ambiguity in predictions.

So what do we do when we lack perfect data? Certainly, it's better to make recommendations when we are very confident the current action will result in a negative outcome. Telling you not to cut your finger off with a knife would be a logical preventive action (as long as other conditions are met, like you aren't stuck on a train track with an oncoming train and only your finger is holding you stationary). Telling you to avoid a particular intersection because there is a multiple-car pileup also seems to make sense. Having your car automatically apply hard braking when a collision is deemed imminent (due to mismatched velocities of your car and the car in front of you) also seems like a good idea, as we know the gulf between reaction times for humans versus computing systems is wide. In this case, taking an action *without* asking makes sense. And those scenarios give us clues about how we deal with a lack of perfect data.

1. Search systems must be able to tell people *why* it makes the decisions it is making for them. The system does not have to always display that information (as in the collision example), but if search does ask for clarification, the question should be expressed in a way that we as humans can understand and base a decision on. This notion of *transparency* is key to helping people trust the new generation of search in the long term.

2. A system must be able to tell users with what confidence it is making a prediction. Noting that there is a

95 percent chance the particular airplane ticket price will fall in the next seven days (something Farecast did when it launched) or that Netflix thinks you will give the movie you are about to watch 3.5 stars helps people both make good decisions and trust the system. Again, it isn't always necessary to show the information—one can imagine a scenario in which the user is driven insane by being given the odds for every action—but it must be available.

3. The known downside risks should be low. Predicting that my girlfriend is available for a Skype call right now based on her schedule and habits is safe because the worst-case scenario—she doesn't answer—isn't that bad. And the upside is that I can talk to her about our upcoming trip.

And why should we expect perfection? One could argue that such measured risk taking is nothing more than an extension of what we humans do every day—we make decisions based on what is likely to generate the best outcomes. All we are doing with the next generation of search is adding more data to the decision-making process. We don't often guard against unknown consequences in our everyday life (indeed, we often maximize immediate pleasure at the expense of long-term happiness). The reason we should expect more from search than we do from our own personal methods of decision making is simple: we need to be able to trust it.

Decision Paralysis and Conformity

As I noted earlier, too much data in decision scenarios actually leads humans to be less happy. When you have many, many choices, the probability that you will be satisfied with your ultimate choice is lower. When search engines of the future get all the data they can process, the way they display that data to users will be critical.

On one side, we will have a user interface that attempts to simplify the entire mass of data into something that can be acted upon in a variety of scenarios. But this has its own risks, one of which is described in *The Filter Bubble* by Eli Pariser— in an attempt to personalize and rationalize the mass of data on the web, engines present information and services believed to be relevant to the user that end up reinforcing the user's existing beliefs. In other words, if someone always chooses Fox News after a news search or always clicks on a particular type of story about an environmental issue, search could, according to the theory, become hyper-personalized, showing the searcher only similar stories and blocking diverse opinions in results. There are a number of issues with this theory despite its logical attractiveness (a paper written by Susan Dumais, Paul Andre, and Jaime Teevan, *From X-Rays to Silly Putty via Uranus: Serendipity and Its Role in Web Search,* refutes the idea that personalization harms search serendipity), but the concern has some foundation. If nothing else, the idea that a search system would return only highly curated results plays into the narrative that people are being controlled by forces they can't see.

A good example that reinforces this fear is a recent study by Robert Epstein and Ronald Robertson at the American Institute for Behavioral Research and Technology titled *Democracy at Risk: Manipulating Search Rankings Can Shift Voters' Preferences Substantially Without Their Awareness.* In the study, Epstein and Robertson describe how they were able to manipulate search results in a way that swayed voter preference toward the favored candidate in significant and predictable directions. What does this mean? Ostensibly, search engines could manipulate public opinion on a variety of topics without users even knowing it's happening.

On the other side, search can present such a panoply of options that users end up in the scenario Dr. Barry Schwartz describes in *The Paradox of Choice*—namely, they constantly second-guess their choices and are dissatisfied with their decisions. Stanford professor Anthony Bastardi talks more about this phenomenon, but broadens it from mere dissatisfaction with one's choice. According to Bastardi, the presence of too much data actually leads people to make worse choices. Says Bastardi: "Decision makers pursue non-instrumental information—information that appears relevant but, if simply available, would have no impact on choice. Once they pursue such information, people then use it to make their decision. Consequently, the pursuit of information that would have had no impact on choice leads people to make choices they would not otherwise have made."[7]

More choices from more data doesn't equate to more happiness.

Clearly, search engines' responsibility to help humans make sense of vast amounts of data is paramount. Far from its humble beginnings as ten blue links, search has become, and will continue to be, critical to making better decisions in a world where we have too many choices. The question is: Can the engines keep up?

Fighting Back:
Big Data Meets Big Computation

There are emerging solutions to the challenges. For example, a company called Ayasdi has developed a cloud-based service called the Insight Discovery Platform. This system is data agnostic, meaning a user can basically throw anything at it and it will attempt to find correlations and derive insights without the user having to ask any questions. The system processes data, discovers the correlations between them, and then displays those results in visualizations that mortals can understand.

For example, imagine trying to learn who the bad actors were in the Enron collapse. Consider parsing twenty thousand employees' e-mails, looking for patterns that might show who knew of the fraud. Ayasdi ran five hundred thousand e-mails through its text analysis solution and was able to identify 205 individuals who likely had relevant information regarding the fraud. By looking for people with similar e-mail content—in particular keywords such as "bankruptcy" and "crisis"—and correlating that with people who sent a lot of e-mails to external accounts with other trigger words, the team was able to sniff out Managing Director for Research Vince Kaminski, who repeatedly raised objections to Enron's shady financial practices. The highlighted subgroup in the figure shows how easy it was for Ayasdi to identify and drill into anomalous data to derive an insight.

In this case, the system doesn't understand the meaning of the correlations, it simply knows that items are connected. Someone still has to figure out which items are important and

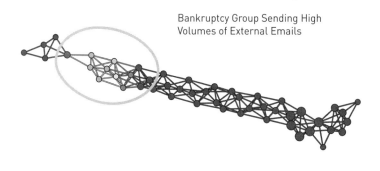

Bankruptcy Group Sending High
Volumes of External Emails

0.0000   250.0000 500.0000
Default

FIGURE 6-1

why, but the ability to inject a data set into a system and have the system find the correlations is a major step in dealing with the deluge of information on the web.

Ayasdi CEO Gurjeet Singh explains, "There are so many questions to ask that you don't have the time to ask them all. It doesn't even make sense to think about where to start your analysis."[8] Indeed, letting search systems find for us what *might* be interesting among the trillions of data points generated by our very existence might be the only way society can get past the immense information overload.

A Glimmer of Hope

Never in human history have we lived in a time when entire parts of our world are upended—relatively routinely—by a few engineers in an office. Think about the impact of Twitter on democracies around the world, or how the Android OS has helped make devices that capture the world insanely cheap. It's unclear whether the creators of disruption had such objectives on their whiteboards when they dreamed up these new products.

And that is what is difficult about predictions in the technology space. One could say, "There are simply too many variables coming from too many directions to allow us to adequately address or even understand all the combinatorial issues that will arise"—and with that I agree. But just as innovation disrupts the status quo, when disruption and the mess it can create *is* the status quo, disruption itself is subject to an upending. I have confidence that even the massive challenges I've described will be solved, if not all at once, at least in an order that moves us toward the next, seemingly impossible set of challenges.

CHAPTER **7**

What Holds Search Back: The Business

We've examined some of the technical challenges facing this next generation of search, which will bestow on us superpowers rivaling those in our wildest science fiction fantasies. But even if we were to completely resolve the technical challenges (which we can never do, as new ones will arise as quickly as we knock down the current ones), there remain issues beyond the technical. Are the business models that fuel search flexible enough to move away from the current practices used to fund these behemoths? Are we able to balance people's rights and freedoms with the access to their information that is required to power these new experiences? Are people already too concerned about the state of their personal information to have serious conversations about *more* access to their data? This chapter seeks to examine those issues.

There's Too Much Money in the System

The stark reality is that online search systems cost *many billions* per year to design, build, and operate. And today the dominant model that funds this R&D relies on text ads on web pages. When we get into the next generation of search, there simply isn't the same arrangement of results on a page or a right column for ads. So how do we balance the need to fund a massive enterprise with the need to advance the state of the art?

In 2013, for example, $50.5 billion of Google's $55.5 billion in revenue came from advertising. This isn't an indictment of the company's model, it's simply a reality. When nearly 91 percent of your revenue (and likely most of your profit) comes from a single source, the willingness to move away from that model is abrogated.

What about models that don't rely on text ads for revenue generation? We have all seen the attempts to shoehorn traditional media advertising models into these online media, from "banners" (really just a small print ad from a magazine or newspaper) to video "pre-rolls" (who doesn't love watching a thirty-second non-targeted clip before the forty-five-second video plays?) or even full-page takeovers. As we move from simple text and video on the web to task completion, models for funding these multibillion dollar expenses will need to evolve. The reality is that these enterprises *need* to generate gargantuan sums if they are to continue to offer their services—and the revenues can be raised either through direct payments from the people who use the services or through some indirect means. Even a relatively small data center of fifty thousand servers costs a minimum of $3.5 million per month to run (assuming a three-year server and ten-year infrastructure amortization), and that's before we even get into the cost of Internet access or the software that runs on them. Something on the scale of Google likely costs well over $15 billion a year to operate.

Better Advertising Isn't More Advertising

You could argue that the perfect ad is one in which the advertiser has high confidence that it will spur the consumer to take action. The action isn't necessarily purchasing a product or a service; billions of dollars are spent on "brand advertising," which seeks to associate an image with a company or product. In any case, advertising is subject to the problem of attribution—basically, it's difficult to separate which of the many potential messages a consumer saw contributed to the desired outcome (whether that's a purchase, a change in perception, raised awareness, etc.).

How could the systems that power search help with a problem like attribution? Ultimately, one could argue that a woven connective fabric in search that understands you, what you're doing in both the physical and virtual worlds, and what you're seeing as you go down your path could be very helpful in linking your actions with the marketing you were exposed to. In other words, in the near future it could be possible to track when you saw a particular ad for the first time, as well as track all the times you've seen it. Or search might note a conversation you had on social media about a product that you bought a week later, after seeing an ad on a digital billboard.

This sounds a little creepy, I realize, and I am not fully convinced the public will welcome such tracking and monitoring for the purpose of helping advertisers understand the return on their ad dollars. But what is the alternative? Today, we have fairly imprecise ways to capture whether an ad has an impact on buying or perceptions. Practices like retargeting make it seem like someone is following you across the web—haven't you noticed that, if you click on a Leggs pantyhose ad on some gossip site, you now see more Leggs pantyhose ads on your e-commerce and other sites? Not only is this silly for me, it's quite out of context if I'm reading an article on CNN about Iran. I foresee next-generation ad models depending on channels being able to bill advertisers for the desired outcome, whether that's a user buying a product or speaking well of the brand to her friends.

Better Advertising Is No Advertising

Another way to potentially resolve the challenge of paying for more advanced search is to have people actually pay for the services they use. Today, everyone pays basically nothing, but even that is lopsided. You might assume that those who use a search service more would generate more profiling data and ad clicks, and thus more revenue to offset the costs they are generating by using the services. In fact, this model has a logic to it, but it's not the only way.

A business model in which users pay for services offers hope for rapid advancement in search.

Indeed, a casual, infrequent searcher who is looking for attorney or medical information will likely generate more money than a heavy searcher who searches for celebrity gossip. Why? The ads on the right side of most search pages are auction based—meaning that some words cost much more than others. And for words involving high potential revenue from a customer (like "medical" or "gambling" or the like), each click can cost the advertiser more than $35. There is nothing wrong with this per se, but it does seem to fly in the face of a usage-based model, because a searcher's volume isn't necessarily correlated with how much revenue they are "paying" to the engine in the form of profile data and ad clicks.

One alternative that has been bandied about for at least fifteen years is the notion of micropayments. Instead of being shown ads as a way to pay for service, a user would pay cents or fractions of a cent for each online task. A search might cost .2 cents, an IM chat might cost .1 cent—in essence, you would be charged for any action you take, just as in many other areas in life. In the same way most people and companies don't provide service for "free," search systems could shift toward collecting payment from users rather than profiling them and exchanging that data for revenue or targeting them with ads. This model is especially attractive to people who look at the collection of data on people as a negative practice with significant potential for abuse. Already, we are seeing that people are willing to pay for ad removal—services like Spotify and Pandora both offer ad-free alternatives, as long as you pay them directly. Recent start-up TrueVault—which recently raised a $2.5 million seed round to provide a HIPAA-compliant API for health-care apps, web apps, and wearables—charges $.001 per data call.

Today, however, search seems too much like oxygen for users to consider paying for it outright. Instead, a growing chorus of industry leaders think that online services can thread the needle to generate needed revenue while preserving privacy and pioneering new models that allow for the next generation of search to prosper.

Rethinking Advertising

Perhaps it's time to rethink how we go about paying for our online services. What if there are ways for advertisers to reach consumers, and thus pay for behemoth systems, without having to use lots of personal data? Again, I want to reinforce that targeted advertising isn't inherently bad—quite the opposite. People report higher satisfaction with search results pages when there are ads on them, as long as they are high quality. But some consumers—and indeed many regulatory bodies—are asking for alternatives to fund the services they love to use.

According to Joe Marchese, CEO of True[x], an advertising technology company, much of the online experience has been stunted by our current advertising models. One example he gave me centered on a television writing class at USC in which the instructor teaches students to write in a three-act format. Why? It isn't because it's the best way to tell a story, it's because they are writing to the commercial breaks. The industry is funded by advertising, so TV shows need to accommodate that ad model. There is no research that shows breaking a story into three parts with cliffhangers to get you to stick around is the best way to handle a narrative arc. Indeed, many of the heralded shows of today are breaking this rule. As Marchese said, "Think about who's winning all the awards right now; Showtime, Cinemax, HBO, Netflix—no ads, no ads, no ads. The only thing that's truly been successful with the traditional ad model and delivered award-winning content today is AMC. If you think about it, a lot of people binge-watch those shows without the ads on Netflix."

Think about this idea as it applies to search. The reason we have what we have today is not because it is necessarily the right model, but because online services like search and e-mail are funded by those contextually relevant ads on the right side of the pages. Are there more effective ways to make sure the companies that fuel search engines can keep the lights on, while benefitting both users and advertisers?

Marchese contends that, especially for certain types of ads, interrupting the flow of a page isn't always the most effective way to capture someone's attention. Marchese says, "I have twenty-four hours in a day. I'm sleeping for about four of them at this point…there is a lot of white space and downtime in those twenty hours when I'm not trying to get something done where I'd be receptive and open to an ad that made sense to me."

Attention bank: a store of engagement credits. You engage with ads when you have time, and apply your accumulated credits when you don't.

Marchese introduced the concept of the "attention bank" to me—in this model, whenever a consumer engages with an ad, he gets a credit.

Those credits could then be used to "pay" for online services. He says:

> People think that the ad needs to be inserted in real time when in reality, you could have a bank. Respect for situational context is something the ad industry is missing. The reason mobile ads are so hard isn't just because the screen is small and the OSs are so fragmented. That's one big reason, but situational context is the primary reason. If I'm going for a run, I don't really care what the advertisement is. Or if I'm trying to find a phone number for a restaurant to call and see if I can get in, please don't interrupt me with an ad. But when I'm out and about, or I'm waiting for a meeting—there are times when I'm receptive to hearing about something I care about. Those are the times when I can bank ad credits—and then when I use the services I want to use, I'm not interrupted.
>
> The ad model needs to adjust to fit the media. Media isn't an evolution; it goes through these fits of revolution. The radio gets invented and then all of a sudden, motion picture is invented, and then broadcast, and then cable, and then YouTube. The media—in this case search systems—will and have evolved first. Advertising will be behind for a period of time because while media's demand-pulled, advertising is supply-managed on the fact that we have so much money in the system. And this is how it flows until something else hits a critical mass.

In other words, we are today seeing innovation in search. Wearables, aural search, visual search, agents—many of these things are advancing the state of the art. But a revolution in search, where we no longer have the familiar interface of links and keywords, requires ad models that can support search being anytime, anywhere, on any device.

Alternative Revenue Models

Another model that appears increasingly likely to help offset the costs of running a large online operation is diversification of revenue streams with the intent of creating a multisided market. If you look at Google's recent financial filings, you see that almost 10 percent of 2013 fourth-quarter revenue came from hardware, applications, and services. That is a profound shift, considering that proportion was in the low single digits just a year earlier. Why the shift? At least for Google, it appears to be a classic multisided market play.

Cross-sided network effects allow you to give something away on one "side" of a market to build network effects that allow you to sell services or products on the other side. Google is "giving away" its operating system for connected devices, which then links users of those inexpensive pieces of hardware to their services, which they monetize by featuring ads. As we have seen with the rise of Android in just four short years, those network effects can create a barrier to entry as, for example, Android begins to achieve huge market share and Google doesn't necessarily have to allow other services on the device. Thus, its "free" product on one side allows it to effectively box out competitors and fully capture all the value on the paid side. In some cases this force is powerful enough to cause a market to "tip" to a single company, at which point it isn't really a market. So while we see diversification in Google's revenue stream, a possible scenario is that it is there less for pure diversification and more to lock in higher-margin online services.

But free services are not simply a way to lock in advertising. Free services can also be an important factor in tapping into the irrational attraction people have to anything that is "free." The web's freemium model—where a user gets something for free but can upgrade to a better version of the service for a fee—could be a solution to generating enough revenue to keep search services humming. We see this model at work today in services like Dropbox, which paid for little advertising but used free storage as a hook to get people to try the product; a quality service and incentives to get users' friends to join made the company's cost of acquiring paying customers far less than it had been when the service launched.

Privacy

While search's advertising-funded business model has spawned incredible innovation and connected hundreds of millions of people to advertisers in an efficient market, the explosion of data and the ubiquity of cheap sensors that can track everything gives some people pause. While users are fine with a search engine presenting ads in relation to a query they typed— after all, Microsoft's internal research shows people like search pages better if there are high-quality ads on the page—they get a little nervous when they see how much data online services have about them. And as we put more of our actions, interests, and ideas into the cloud, that ability to profile will only grow.

Marc Davis, one of the preeminent thinkers about digital selves, raises an interesting point about how much data we have online:

Let's say we've got roughly a million years that we've been homo sapiens, give or take, and so we've got a million years of experience, phenomenology, and cultural practice around what it means to be a physical self, a physical person. Cultures deal with it differently, but proxemics—how close you stand to people, how we organize ourselves in dwellings, and the rest—we've got a tremendous amount of knowledge and experience with being physical persons.

About ten thousand years ago, depending on how you count it or if you want to go back to the *Code of Ur-Nama,* which was actually before Hammurabi, we had the notion of a legal person, which defined what you can do and what you can't do, and so you had a level of affordance or structure on behavior and action.

Now, in the last fifteen years, a new type of person has been created, *the digital person,* and what hasn't been sorted out yet is exactly what that's going to be, who's going to control it, and what the relationships are between the digital person, the legal person, and the physical person. So many questions are swirling—on surveillance, access to data, who owns your information, who can see you when and where.

Our digital selves need to be protected, just like our physical selves.

The fundamental questions, privacy and control, are really about the nature of personhood, and so if you look at it in large historical terms, from physical person to legal person to digital person, all three of them coexist. They're all relating to each other in complex ways and we're at the very, very beginning of sorting this out. It's going to be a long historical process, but the things that get determined even in the next few years are going to have massive effects going forward.

When looking at the current state of our personal data it is easy to view the major Internet players as pseudo-state actors. As much of what had been public infrastructure is replaced by web or mobile services (that is, paper mail is replaced with e-mail and Facebook, federally controlled airwaves are augmented by Twitter, and so on), the companies that operate these services begin to look like quasi-public institutions. The problem, of course, is that they aren't run like public institutions.

This is not to say that there is malicious intent on their part with respect to people's private data, but the mere fact that legislation barely exists to govern the storage and use of that data in the public realm means we are likely much further away from having safeguards in place in the privatized town square.

Technical, Social, Personal, and Societal Dimensions

Privacy is a huge piece of kryptonite threatening to hold back a quantum leap in search. Many view a world in which a powerful agent knows a great deal about us as suspect and unwanted. The paradox is that the freedom this new world will endow us with is predicated on us giving away more of our information. The big data systems of today work better with more data, and their ability to act on our behalf is abrogated when we close pieces of that data off. So how do we resolve this paradox? There are a number of issues to consider, and they range from technical to social, societal to personal.

The technical hurdles to collecting and using personal data are probably the easiest to overcome. For all intents and purposes, storage is essentially free. Computation is very, very cheap—so the ability to cross-correlate personal data points is inexpensive. The most expensive part of the system is likely the data scientists and developers who form the insights and resulting algorithms that are applied to the mass of data in order to make sense of it and add value to peoples' lives.

More problematic than the technical aspect are societal attitudes toward enabling higher-order search, and expert systems in general, to have a view into every area of people's lives. We are, however, seeing changing attitudes toward what people do online and an increased willingness to share data—especially in the younger demographic. From the Pew Research Center in 2012:

Overall, 40 percent of teen social media users say they are "very" or "somewhat" concerned that some of the information they share on social networking sites might be accessed by third parties like advertisers or businesses without their knowledge. However, few report a high level of concern; 31 percent say that they are "somewhat" concerned, while just 9 percent say that they are "very" concerned. Another 60 percent in total report that they are "not too" concerned (38 percent) or "not at all" concerned (22 percent).

According to Ben Livshits, a lead thinker about privacy issues, one of the key challenges is that we, as consumers of search services, can't understand the value of our information. In other words, we are used to getting services for free, but the reality is that there is no such thing as free. There has to be some sort of value exchange to fund the multibillion-dollar infrastructure required to power this new generation of online services. Today, that is paid for when companies "monetize" their users' profiles—for example, systems know I am a male, in my late thirties, likely live in Seattle, and have a number of attributes that make me attractive to a certain class of advertiser or to a function inside a service designed to drive retention. The most fiscally productive online companies understand the value of *me* knowing all this profile data because they can constantly test and validate whether what they believe about me—and thus my value to their advertisers—is true. But we consumers are not very good at understanding the value of our information.

How Much Is My Privacy Worth?

Today, consumers have no real way of understanding what their information is worth. Companies like BlueKai and their

Registry product attempt to let anybody see what online advertisers likely know about them. Others services, like PrivacyFix, offer an estimate of your worth to major online services like Google and Facebook. But a granular understanding of your true online worth to the myriad sites you visit in a day is elusive. As more revelations about data collection creep into the public consciousness, awareness seems to be increasing.

According to Livshits:

> I think we are starting to calibrate the value of [our] information, and we're doing that very, very slowly, sort of bit by bit by bit. I think this is generally a discovery process. We really do not know, much of the time, how much people value things like name and phone number, not to mention preferences such as what kind of movies they prefer to watch, and what kind of channels they tend to watch on Comcast. I think figuring out what that is will take some time, and I think much of the time it's basically a dance around a service, saying, "Well, I'll give you this in exchange for that." And especially when it's a free service, you'll give your value away.

The current model of funding innovation relies on companies using personal data to make more revenue than it costs to provide their service. This isn't a bad thing, necessarily—it just is.

And it's not just about money. There is a desire to create something that appeals to the end users—something personalized and useful for them—which is very difficult to do without knowing anything about them! So we risk people becoming less interested in having their data mined as they feel the value of their information is worth more than the service they're receiving. Yet even more data mining is likely required to accomplish a quantum leap in the technology of search. It will be a rare company that feels an incentive to quantify how much a user's information is worth to them. Today, companies don't have to. They can offer as little or as much value to the consumer as they wish, and there is no bargaining.

The second that I, as a consumer, know that my address or my preferences are worth $4 to a service, the whole dynamic of the industry changes. Livshits equates the current state of the market to the Grand Bazaar in Istanbul, in that there are likely twenty-five sellers for any given item, and unless you haggle you won't know the real "value" of the object. Consider comparison-shopping engines, a fairly recent invention that popped up to serve the needs of an inefficient marketplace: before such engines, you would have to visit a number of websites or call physical locations to compare pricing. Today, that task has largely been automated by any number of sites.

> Are consumers getting enough value from companies in exchange for their personal data?

In Focus: A Potential Solution—RePriv

Ben Livshits designed a system, called RePriv, that attempts to overcome some of the privacy issues that concern users. This research project is all about presenting the user with options for what to share when visiting a website or using a service. RePriv sits quietly on your device and monitors your Internet and local machine activities. It sounds scary but it's not—it's yours and no one else's. The whole point is to create a membrane between your information and the sites that request it. For example, if I want to visit the website for HarrysWidgetShop.com, RePriv intercepts requests from the site for information about me. It then displays a dialog box that asks me what, if any, information I would like to share, and I decide the level I'm comfortable with. I could choose to share my gender but not my zip code, for example.

The challenge gets obvious pretty quickly. Users are not good at understanding the complexity of the information they consent to give, for a couple of reasons: (1) the sheer volume of requests would overload even the savviest users as they traverse the web and (2) users wouldn't really understand the marginal value of sharing a piece of information on top of what they've already shared. In other words, my zip code might be worth $4 to an advertiser and my car model might be worth $.50 on its own. But when an advertiser combines the two, the value could very well be more than $4.50—in fact, it could be much, much higher because the ability to run correlations on these data against other data sets might yield insights that either piece of information in isolation wouldn't generate.

RePriv would be able to act as that intelligent broker, serving as a marketplace for your personal data and performing as an agent that intercepts requests from sites and services that want information about you for various purposes. In some cases it would give the information away for free (when Uber needs to know my location to send a car, for instance), but in others it might decide that, before it releases my height to an airline (presumably to upsell a business class seat), it will find out what the airline knows about me and the likely value of my information to the airline, and then broker the value of my information *for me*.

It is a monumentally difficult thing to contemplate building. Price transparency (i.e., how much you are worth to a site or service) is nil. There isn't even a standard system that all your web transactions go through. Some are on your PC, others on your mobile, others on a cheap tablet, others on a connected device with no screen. Without a single identity

and a single broker system that lives in the cloud—and which
all the sites and services on the web agree to use—it seems
we will be left with a piecemeal solution for the foreseeable
future.

Let's assume for a moment that we do build a service like
RePriv that operates in the cloud and functions across the
web. The other major issue we face is the question of imputed
data. In other words, I may let a system know my age and my
marital status, but then what about the insights it derives and
stores based on those variables such as my likelihood to buy
an expensive vacation, or if I'm likely to be a good target for
a dating site ad? Who owns that data? What if my marital
status changes or what if I no longer want to report my sexual
preference but a system has already built a profile based on my
prior granting of that data?

Marc Davis has a solution grounded in the real world:
Hollywood.

We produce and sell movies and then have the most
complex rights clearances imaginable. Thousands of
different parties in a film can have rights: the music
guys, the dance people, products in the movie...there
are just incredibly complex contracts that govern the
various rights associated with that complex artifact—
a movie. When you think about personal data, there's
a three by three matrix that I developed to help inform
who *owns* what. On the left, it's about ownership: some
stuff is completely, solely mine; then there is stuff that's
joint or has shared rights among multiple parties; and
then there is stuff that's public, meaning it's in the public
domain or used for public good, so no one owns it or
everyone owns it.

On the top, it's about data. There's declared data, or things that are explicitly stated. Next, observed data comes from devices that track you; finally, we have inferred data, or data that is computed based on a number of things systems know about you. So you've got a nice three by three matrix, but it shows that most of the data out there is jointly, not solely, owned.

	Declared Data	Observed Data	Inferred Data
Solely Mine	Sole Ownership	Joint Ownership	Joint Ownership
Owned by Multiple Parties	Joint Ownership	Joint Ownership	Joint Ownership
Owned by No One (Public Domain)	Joint Ownership	Joint Ownership	Joint Ownership

The reality is that, while, yes, it's my data and I do own it and have rights to it, I'm not the only one who does.

So it seems that we have an answer without an actual solution. Yes, search systems can recognize that there is some data that I don't own and that can be used to aim both services and ads toward me. But, unlike in Hollywood, there is no solution to the problem of what happens to imputed data when I say, "This is data I no longer want known to online services,"— my age, for example. Online companies must focus on how they can "back out" imputed data when one or more of the components they used to compute their profile data is no longer accessible.

Data: Yours, Mine, and Ours

This realization that we don't actually own all the data about us stored on the web points to the need for legal and technical architecture supports that are "tracking, identifying, and arbitrating amongst the rights of multiple parties who have rights to the data," according to Marc Davis.

In the overall data picture that describes you, it is likely that the majority of data is governed by multiple parties. At that point, the industry or government must assert fundamental rights around how each of these parties can use, store, and delete this data.

At the very least, an individual's right to access what a system knows about her will likely need to be available in this near-future web. The complexity of data rights also bodes well for systems like RePriv or personal clouds, because in those types of systems *you* own all your data and you at least have a record of who knows what about you and what they might have done with your data. Such systems wouldn't wholly solve the shared or imputed ownership issue, but at least in theory a user could run analytics against his own digital persona to understand his likely value and exposures.

Personal Clouds

In response to what they view as an invasion of privacy by services they use, some people have created their own "personal clouds." Broadly defined, these clouds are either servers users host in their homes (for the geeks) or private cloud storage that only they have access to.

Services like Tonido turn any machine you own into a system you can access from anywhere. Unlike with Dropbox or Google Drive, with Tonido the data doesn't leave your possession—so there is nothing for an engine to analyze—at least not without your express permission. Alternatives include companies like Rackspace, FireHost, and others that allow users to pay for cloud storage to which only they have access.

Those who have fled to personal clouds have concluded, or at a minimum *reacted* to the fact, that they don't know where or how their data is being used. Rather than carefully controlling their personal data permissions, an arduous task that takes a lot of time, they have simply built a wall around their data.

People are also now building private social networks, either on servers in their own homes or on hosted solutions to which only a few people have access. Of course, hosting social networks on a server in your home seems to defeat the purpose of being social, but I digress. While such networks may be less social in that only those invited can participate, they are also ostensibly much less prone to being mined for profile-building purposes.

In any case, the rise of personal clouds as a response to security and privacy concerns dramatically affects how search can use data to maximize a personally relevant search experience. If people feel that the only way to remain secure on the web is to lock their information in digital safes away from prying eyes, the ability for intelligent systems to access and harness that data for the user's benefit will of course be hampered.

Terms of Servi(tude)

Would you allow a person you didn't know to babysit your young child without explicit laws against bad behavior and recourse when people break those laws? Kidnapping is illegal, driving kids around without a seatbelt is illegal, giving children cigarettes is illegal in the U.S. There is a social contract that holds communities together and allows people to put themselves in a position of calculated risk because there is an assurance of recourse if the contract is broken.

Marc Davis, the computer scientist and thinker we met earlier, is also a founding member of the World Economic Forum's Rethinking Personal Data Project, and he has a lot to say about the state of consumers' rights on the Internet:

There's an effort called TOSDR.org, Terms of Service; Didn't Read, which is working to promote transparency around privacy on the Internet. Their main contention is

that "I have read and agree to the Terms" is the biggest
lie on the web. And they aim to fix that.

What they've done is analyze the various Terms of Service from many different Internet companies and they've
typified and classified what those agreements asked for and
then rated them. What they also realized when they did
this was (a) no one reads these things, (b) their hair would
fall out if they realized what they're agreeing to, and (c) it's
different with almost every party they're dealing with. You
have this massively inefficient, very asymmetrical system.
You have almost what in legal terms is called a contract
of adhesion. A contract of adhesion is a one-way, non-
negotiable contract in which the parties have asymmetrical
power and so you're going to have to agree or else.

Davis's main point is simple: we have constitutionally
protected rights like freedom of speech, freedom from self-
incrimination, freedom from unreasonable search and seizure,
and more. Today, many of the places where we communicate
with others are increasingly "owned" by nonstate actors. In
other words, we have protection of speech as we stand atop a
soapbox in the middle of a public street, able to talk to everyone within earshot, but that public square is increasingly moving online, to one that has a different sets of rights based on
the platform's terms of service.
Private companies increasingly
perform many of the functions
that the state once did, and
which are no longer available
from the state. According to
Davis: "Private entities are not beholden to protect freedom of
speech and, in fact, require you to give up a variety of constitutionally protected rights in order to use their private services."

The "public square" is
increasingly moving online,
to sites owned by nonstate
actors.

Initiatives being drafted, especially in the European Union, focus on new rights of individuals asserted over these private companies that will extend the protections granted to us in the public sphere because, as Davis says, "so much of the public sphere is now technically provided by the private sphere."

Other ideas, like a single terms of service agreement for the web, will have profound implications if implemented. If online services protect our data and don't have any hidden surprises in their TOS (because they're all using the same one), we no longer have to read the TOS each time and would be afforded the same protections from service to service. Davis says, "Ideally, [a single terms of service] will be supported by the European Union and vetted over and against the coming Data Regulations. So we would end up with a contract that is *truly* two way between people and the organizations that manage their information for them; and that protects the rights of the individual over and against both the state and the private sectors. It is one of the most important things we can do."

This work will increase trust in the systems, shining light into the areas of the internet most people don't understand. Once people know what they are agreeing to and have confidence that their rights as individuals are protected, they'll be more comfortable fully embracing intelligent search systems that can work on their behalf.

A First-Class Web?

One potential solution to the dilemma of exchanging privacy for services is to create a class of sites or services for which there is an impetus for both parties to be honest, creating a premium experience on the web. Today, we are all engaged in a dance of data. I might report my birthday as one date on a particular site and as a different date on another. At the same time, sites and services may tell me they are using my data in one way, but the end result is something quite different.

Again, Livshits says:

> What if we were to elevate the level of this conversation a little bit, which is to say, I'm actually going to give you genuine information about myself. If in return for your accurate information you got something tangible, and that developed not into just a one-off thing, but a long-term engagement with somebody on the other side that would be open to auditing by your agent, just like any financial relationship is, everybody in that exchange would be highly incentivized to be above the table and on the books and everything else. I'm going to tell you information, and if you really want to audit the correctness of the information, you are welcome to do so. I'm really on the up and up, but in return, I expect the same.

In this scenario there would be a mutually beneficial relationship between the user and the web service, just as we currently have with our financial institutions. The agreement is that I give the institution information like my birthdate and the city where I live (and a bunch of other information) to get a mortgage, and I trust the bank will count my money accurately and keep a record of my payments. This sort of high-touch, premium relationship might be one way to keep the privacy demons at bay at least for a class of sites and services on the web like search that require personal information to function well.

A Solution: Sunlight

I believe many of the privacy and data use issues can be overcome by acknowledging them fully and exposing them to the light. What won't work is rushing ahead, consequences be damned (the tendency of many in the technology industry).

Privacy, security, and the individual's value as a digital citizen are critical issues that cannot be left undefended.

There are good actors today working to prevent overreach in the areas of privacy and personal data from becoming pervasive and persistent problems. There are others who say we've already gone too far and that trying to restore privacy as we knew it, for example, is a lost cause. Instead, they say, we need to construct models of thinking that accept our new normal. Just as people had to get used to traffic lights on streets, they need to concede certain realities about privacy in today's world; technical advancements come with new requirements, but these are ultimately to the benefit of society.

In any case, the only thing we can really agree on is that we must work on these issues now. Ignoring them and hoping they will simply resolve themselves through continued technical advancement is a recipe for disaster. As I've mentioned, I'm a techno-optimist. I believe wholeheartedly that my colleagues in the technology arena are working in good faith toward imbuing society with the power of omniscient wisdom, and that together we can counter the bad actors who turn up in any system. Our final chapter will explore just what this new society might look like.

CHAPTER **8**

A Time to Believe

Let's assume for a moment that all the challenges of privacy, security, technical capacity and aptitude, and funding that we've explored are resolved. It's a stretch, perhaps, but walk with me for a moment. Many of the challenges seem intractable and certainly not for the faint of heart: Disrupting multibillion dollar enterprises that spin off billions of dollars a year in revenue and shareholder value? Embracing the complexity of a digital self while ensuring personal data is used appropriately and with proper precautions? Building new hardware and software architectures necessary to both consume and process the increasingly digital world?

Any one of these dilemmas could be a lifetime's work, with no guarantee of success. But what if we pull ourselves out of the current technical stall and move search into the realm of its full potential, rather than just accepting what it is? What could a search system do?

In this final chapter, we'll conduct a short thought experiment where we'll stop for a moment and examine a higher purpose of search, looking at what could happen both culturally and societally, assuming we knock down the most complex issues facing search today and embrace search as the hinge that will make us better versions of ourselves.

Digitizing You: The Real Quantified Self

Today, measuring characteristics of one's movements or sleep patterns seems to be all the rage. Certainly, there are huge benefits to this: motivation to move more for healthy living and optimal sleep cycles, better understanding of caloric consumption, and the ability to compare these data to demonstrate progress against one's self and others. In other words, people are willing to digitally store personal information when there is a *clear benefit to them.* Can you imagine in the past some system asking you every day how many steps you walked? Your first question would have been "Why the heck should I tell you?" It wasn't until there was a clear benefit to volunteering that piece of personal information that people—tens of millions of them—bought fitness-tracking wearables like Fitbit, Nike+ FuelBand, and Jawbone UP.

The same process will occur with the rest of our physical data—as we see a value to sharing information, we'll be willing to make more of our data available. The challenge that the technical community must solve—in addition to the privacy issues—is *why* people should allow systems access: those of us involved in the tech world need to build a case for the true digital self. We need to paint a picture of what a comprehensive understanding of humanity could generate for all society. The alternative is to follow the current model of gradual, ad hoc digitization of different pieces of our selves, complete with altitude mismatches (we in the digital world know very little about human genomic makeup and entirely too much about people's movie viewing habits) and varying levels of privacy controls. It will take far too long for us to piece together value propositions for every fragment of our selves to be captured and stored for later use. Rather, we need to more aggressively digitize *everything* about ourselves to see the truths hiding in the data that we, as humans, can't process.

In my technological utopia, I want us to have a single digital warehouse for our entire self. Every personal characteristic, derived and explicit, would be captured and controlled by its "owner." What would that look like?

- I never have to repeat myself. If I tell a system that I like window seats on airplanes, I never want to have another system ask about that again... unless my actions routinely contradict my explicit declaration. If I say I like window seats but constantly override my reserved seat or change to an aisle seat once I get on the plane, the system should not ignore that, but ask me if what it knows is really accurate, updating my profile if necessary.
- All my implicit actions on any device are stored and modeled. My system will know I am presented with connections through Denver when I'm flying to Florida, but that I never pick them. In other words, it understands what I am thinking by watching what I am doing on my devices and saves that information for later use. I never want to have to see options through Denver because I will never pick it... unless there are no other options that meet my needs.
- My entire genome and health information are saved and updated with regularity. When did I last get a cold? When did I suffer from high levels of cortisol? At what time of day did my pulse-ox level drop? Rather than merely counting steps, we could open up an entirely new ability to live a healthier life with little effort through a truly quantified self. Is your blood sugar getting low? Do you tend to become sleepy and unproductive when this happens? Should a system alert you to eat an orange when your blood sugar drops so you can avoid that situation?
- Information about every friend I have and every acquaintance I've ever met is collected. Imagine if every text or

WhatsApp conversation with every person you know was stored for later analysis. A search system that can identify who your friends are and what they mean to you could help you out of a jam or might expand your thinking on a question, and this could deepen human relations through higher-quality conversations and experiences.

The ability to see real and potential connections among and between people would open up a much higher yield for all interactions. Imagine you meet someone, have an interesting conversation about tigers in Africa, and see that person again the following year at the same conference. What if you had had a conversation with someone funding research into those tigers at some point during the year? Wouldn't it be magic if you were reminded of that fact when you saw your acquaintance at the conference? Think of all the good we could do if we effortlessly recalled and passed along contacts and information that others in our network might find valuable in their lives and work.

In addition to systems understanding our whole selves, the sensors all around us would allow the systems to understand even more of the things that contribute to our "real" self. Imagine if you never again had to capture a receipt for a return or remember what you bought last month or worry about what you had for dinner last night interacting with a medication you were scheduled to take today. In a quantified reality, brought to us by the proliferation of inexpensive devices that report and analyze the real world, it would be a simple matter to keep track of:

- Everything I buy and everything I return, in every size and color and style, with all that information synthesized into a model that resembles my true interests and likes

- Everything I read online and off; how often I actually finish the book rather than stop reading halfway through
- Everywhere I go, when, and for how long (with current sensors)
- Everything I eat and drink, when and how often (with new sensors)
- Everything I see, how each thing makes me feel, and who I engage with in real life

And so much more. The point? What we consider our digital self today is a shadow of what is yet to come. Our ability to truly understand ourselves and the environment in which we live, and therefore have our systems serve our interests, is on the cusp of becoming more than science fiction.

A More Digitized World

The world is racing toward mass digitization, but the technology industry can do more to encourage a higher-fidelity world in less time. Put another way, the industry can provide incentives for producers of content to contribute more of their information and services to the digital web, and we can make it easier for consumers to contribute their observations and behaviors, which helps model the physical world.

Digitizing by Producers

The first step in leveraging the new web's capabilities is for some new player to build business models that encourage content and service producers to more fully digitize their wares. Entirely new companies will build viable business models that incent producers to put *everything* online. Here are just a few examples of possible uses, to inspire your imagination:

- Farmers' markets see potential new customers when they use computer vision to monitor stock levels at their stands, providing real-time inventory to search systems.
- Hotels use inexpensive RFID-embedded devices to help guests find the mugs or help housekeeping find the outdoor cushions for the balcony.
- Retail stores leverage customers' mobile devices to generate real-time maps of the customer's location within their premises, to help route people where they want to go more efficiently.
- Producers of craft goods use new high-resolution 3D scanning to give potential customers better views of their wares, even offering printed 3D prototypes using home 3D printers.
- Utilities and cities equip their workforces and properties with inexpensive sensors to measure everything from power grid status to crosswalk light timing at lunchtime.
- Industrial manufacturers use state-of-the-art components from companies like GE to provide efficiencies but also real-time status to downstream suppliers.
- Local shops that don't have a massive web presence use cheap and easy webcams to digitize menus, hours of operation, and services; they might also use a $99 tablet to turn those pictures into real-point-of sale systems, complete with the ability to project sales and inventory.

These are just a few examples—you could likely come up with dozens more as you think about your everyday interactions with the physical world and commercial interests in it. The important thing to remember, however, is that there must be aligned incentives for producers. Every second that producers spend quantifying their businesses is a second taken away from running the core business. In many cases, digitizing their work is of unquestionable benefit to their operations, but in some cases tapping into an increasingly digitized world and having other digital actors (quantified citizens and other producers) able to build on top of their work is key to a viable model.

Digitizing by Consumers and Citizens

The second half of the equation in getting to a fully digitized world is allowing consumers to passively and actively model the real world. It has been happening for a decade—think of Yelp and Foodspotting—which allow people to take what they see and know about the real world and put it into a form that can be used by machines and other humans. But the process is currently too complex and costly. Production by users still falls under the Wikipedia rule: about 2 percent create and the rest consume.

For the world to be translated into silicon in the near future, we need to leverage passive consumer capturing of their surroundings. I want everyone's footprints and digital emissions stored forever but also able to be used in real time. This capability might take shape in several forms; for example, think of:

- **Always-listening devices on your body that capture and make sense of your conversations.** For instance, you are sitting in a vegetarian restaurant in rural Vietnam and you tell your girlfriend how amazing the food is. Chances are, you will never rate this place on Yelp, even if you could even remember the name—but that conversation could be recorded and digitized (or even captured locally on your device), then sanitized, synthesized, and sent to the cloud, so others know that a spot at that particular latitude and longitude has good vegetarian food.
- **Visual capturing of everything you see and its location.** Several devices do just that, including Bill Buxton's

LifeCam and the new Autographer product, which captures not just what you're seeing but highlights the interesting stuff along with your entire context, such as location, time of day, direction, and more. Uploading that information and tagging it with data that provides more context would contribute massively to efforts to reconstruct the world in digital form.

- **Next-generation sensors to measure noise levels in physical places** (restaurants, hotels, trains, parks—anywhere).
- **Double validation of producers' inputs to the systems.** Even if the produce stall at the farmers' market reports having plenty of avocado, a quick shot from the neck cam of a shopper in the area might prove otherwise.
- **Real-time data, using a combination of sensors to report to search systems.** Data can include just how long the line at Starbucks is...or how long the wait at the Emergency Room.
- **Biofeedback sensors that could help understand what you love and dislike.** Imagine search understanding what book (or even what part of a book) you really enjoyed by monitoring your heart rate or respiration through simple body-worn sensors. Or think of Kinect being able to measure your heart rate while you are watching a movie. Information gleaned from these passive signals would allow systems to construct amazingly personalized recommendations when you're looking for the next thing to read or watch.
- **Sensors embedded in cars and devices that track speed and location.** Such sensors would answer the age-old question of how much faster the back road is than the highway at this time of day.
- **Simple chemical sampling devices** that help you and others understand how various foods affect blood sugar in people with your particular biochemical makeup.

- **Sensors on your shoes or body** that could identify and report on the cracks in the sidewalk in your neighborhood.

You get the idea. The main question (and opportunity) is this: How can we tap into the constant motion of humanity using the explosion of inexpensive sensors that, much like our natural human senses, see the world around us, albeit at staggeringly high fidelity? And, importantly, how can we translate that information for our digital systems, helping those systems understand the possibilities and restrictions afforded to us by our physical surroundings?

The Control Loop

Among the most interesting things Jeremy Conrad of Lemnos Labs said to me when I interviewed him was that one of the reasons hardware has become so cheap to manufacture is that almost everything made now features a "control loop." He meant that, rather than building precise machines with high fault-tolerance (which increased costs of manufacture), manufacturers can produce less-expensive versions combined with cheap sensors that measure faults in the system. In the old days, a manufacturer or operator wouldn't get feedback from a system until it was so out of alignment that its issues were noticed by humans. The ability to measure the life left on your spark plugs was arbitrary at best; basically, it was only measured when your mechanic checked them (and really, how often is that?). Today, engines take hundreds of measurements every second that can indicate malfunctions *before* they become a problem.

Because all our machines and many of our systems are no longer one-way clients but organisms with the ability to report real-time status, our ability to course correct in real time is unprecedented. Imagine the digitized self and the digitized world, and now imagine we could detect anomalies in all these digital people, places, and things as they are happening. A few scenarios excite me here:

- Traffic lights could modulate automatically in response to congestion or heavy pedestrian load.
- Even the smallest shop would know when to order more inventory of a certain product, as the point-of-sale system would build predictive models based on sell-through.
- With a fully mapped genome and advances in systems biology, combined with an encyclopedic knowledge of ingredients in the food you eat and how it interacts with an individual's biochemistry, systems could offer constant modifications to your diet.
- Smart appliances (like washers and dryers) will talk to the power grid and, rather than running exactly when you tell them, they will turn on when power is cheapest and the grid is least congested.
- Educational models will change in real time based on the way individual students learn. Sites like Khan Academy already enable teachers to see where a particular student is getting stuck in his classwork, letting teachers tailor instruction to the student's needs. This type of real-time pedagogical modification using systems is not far away.

Now, real-time modification of future actions based on historical data isn't a new concept. You can think about it as an advance in a process called "A/B testing," which we use in technical product development all the time. In A/B testing, we launch two versions of a product concept and determine which one performs better against our goals. The winner sticks around and the loser goes back to the drawing board. But this type of testing—through control loops in hardware that can modify operating parameters if new information shows how it can be made more efficient—can now be applied to the physical world. And, more excitingly, the time between data collection and resulting action is dramatically reduced.

The Implications on Life, the Universe, and Everything

At this point you may be (1) nerding out, imagining a world in which things work as they should, your every wish is anticipated, and the pace at which experiences and lives improve increases exponentially, (2) freaking out, running to the nearest store to buy tinfoil with which to wrap your head, your house, and your pets in an attempt to block the coming "great society," or (3) utterly confused and/or skeptical that this new world of search is possible or desirable.

Remember, this chapter assumes we resolve the biggest privacy, technical, and social challenges. It assumes that a complete digital self comes without risk of massive identity theft or an invasion of privacy. It assumes companies can return shareholder value while building these complex, multibillion-node systems. With these assumptions in place, let's take a look at some of the implications of a world made better through increased digitization.

Personal Implications

This symbiosis, or hinge, between humans and machines will generate a healthier, more fulfilled, and better functioning person. As a species, we will have more time for leisure, fewer disappointments as our actions go awry less often, and more confidence in our decisions. Let's explore some potential implications the hinge has for each and every one of us.

Efficiency As the Key to Happiness

Maybe it's my German heritage, but I find little more exciting than making my life more efficient. The reality of our thought experiment is that a fully digitized self and world could dramatically reduce inefficiencies in nearly every interaction we have with people, places, and things.

But I'm often reminded by my mother that increased efficiency isn't the only goal. She'd ask, "Is efficiency all there is? What about enjoyment of life and the pursuit of happiness? What about serendipity?" And to that I say, it depends on *why* we want to achieve peak efficiency. If efficiency produces mainly more rigid constructs in a society governed by data-driven probabilities and rules, and it removes serendipity and discovery from our lives, then it isn't what we want. If reaching peak efficiency chiefly speeds up our lives so we can increase our yield of widgets, the answer is again, no.

But I see efficiency differently. To me, greater efficiency means that we have more time to breathe, to think, and to do things we want to do. Far from becoming automatons, we will be free of the shackles of the mundane.

No one wants to manage a complex daily calendar that includes commuting, remembering appointments and tasks, mailing a package at the post office, and other responsibilities large and small. No one wants to measure the UV index before deciding what to wear. No one aches to spend thirty minutes browsing through a hundred bad direct-to-Netflix movies to find the one gem that might bring joy or insight to a Friday night.

A level of search and digitization that automates such tasks and streamlines our days can unleash boundless curiosity and creativity in society. If a system prompts me to leave at a certain time so I can make it to my daughter's soccer game, I no longer have to expend mental energy tracking the time as

I'm working. Contrary to popular belief, we humans actually *cannot* multitask. We don't do two things at once—we do two things at two different times in close temporal proximity. Worse, we are only able to hold between five and nine items in short-term memory, meaning that if you are thinking about checking traffic so you don't miss the game, you are taking away one or more slots that otherwise could be used to complete your task. Freeing us from having to "time slice" every second of every day means we can focus on completing tasks that require our full brain power—which means ultimately that we have more free time to watch *Real Housewives of Atlanta* if that's what we want to do.

And that brings me to the "Clay Shirky effect." Dr. Shirky is a professor at NYU and one of the smartest people I know. He once posited that "Americans spent two hundred billion hours of their time per week watching TV. To put this into perspective, the entire database on Wikipedia is estimated to have taken just one hundred million hours to complete. This means that this country spends a Wikipedia's worth of time every weekend just watching ads!" In other words, we could literally create a Wikipedia a week if we were truly efficient. But he claims we won't do that, that we are passive consumers most of the time. And he is right. But I want to propose an alternative: What if we weren't so exhausted managing the chuff of everyday cognition? Would we feel the need to switch off at night and crush a *House of Cards* marathon? It's interesting to consider that we might have time to engage in more creative thought if we didn't expend so much energy managing minutiae.

The End of Information Asymmetry

Search has the potential to be a great equalizer for those with access to it. One of the most interesting implications of this next generation of search technologies is a reduction in information asymmetry. Why is this profound? A well-functioning capitalist economic system is predicated on all actors in a transaction having access to the same-level of data. In other words, markets work best when both the buyer and seller can value a good or service fairly. When the party on one side of the transaction has more or better information, that party is able to exploit the imbalance to gain a better deal. The 2001 Nobel Prize in Economics was awarded to economists who pioneered much of the modern research in this space, showing how information asymmetry can cause market failures in the worst cases of exploit, but generally causes people to make less than optimal decisions millions of times per day.

One simple example demonstrates how information asymmetry causes economic harm: consider the question of buying an extended warranty for a car. The buyer (in this case, likely the less informed party) is presented with an option to spend several thousand dollars to extend the warranty on his car by some number of years. How does he make this decision? Certainly, the pricing models presented by the dealer take into account historical performance of the car, meaning how often the car requires service after the main warranty expires. The buyer likely doesn't have that information and therefore makes a decision to buy or not to buy based on arguments made by the seller (the average cost of repairs on this car is $1,200 for electrical systems, and those tend to go out after year four) rather than a true statistical model of the likelihood of failure.

> Search can equalize access to knowledge, making markets more efficient.

Combine that lack of information with the time value of money (how much could the buyer make on the $2,000 he would spend on the warranty if he invested it for four years?), and you can see how pernicious information asymmetry can be. It isn't that extended warranties are bad or good—that is not the point. It isn't that the buyer can't make a decision in his best interest in the current model. It may indeed be important to buy the warranty because data from the car's on-board computers (OBD) demonstrates failures in pricey electronics modules as the cars age, but not having the full picture puts the buyer at a disadvantage. Conversely, it may be that only headlight washer modules fail on this car, in which case the buyer would be spending a lot of money to protect against a relatively inexpensive repair.

Now imagine this scenario in the age of data and search-driven insights. Cars could be (and increasingly are) augmented with an ability to communicate the status and health of their systems to the cloud. Even if manufacturers didn't enable this by default, a piece of hardware could be developed to interface with cars' on-board computers, which could then communicate with a company that analyzed the real-time data coming from cars to determine—just as we do with other predictive analytics—what is likely to happen to a given model over a particular period of time. For example, the system could detect something as simple as a suboptimal mix of oxygen and fuel in the injection chamber for that specific model. This fact by itself might not be interesting, but when it's combined with data from hundreds of thousands of other cars, it may portend a more serious fuel system problem (based on data gleaned from cars that had this injection chamber issue and later developed a more serious condition); timely maintenance could forestall a more serious problem if the driver had all the relevant information. Or, in the case of extended warranties, perhaps this collection of data informs the buyer that taking the warranty makes sense given the likely failures in this model of car.

You can see how search technologies have the potential to make markets work better and to generally make people's lives better. The potential ranges from the mundane—you should question your mechanic's brake replacement recommendation because his friend is the brake part distributor—to the profound—your genome reveals you are likely to develop Parkinson's.

Spotting the Trees in the Forest

Another interesting role for search arises from its potential to unearth bad actors based on latent traces they leave across the digital landscape. As we discussed earlier, the beauty of search technologies is that they can find things in the data that we humans can't see. Our earlier example—and not one in which bad actors are in play—showed the retail chain Target calculating a young woman's pregnancy even before she told her father. Though the teenaged daughter lived with her parents, and they ostensibly knew what she was generally doing, it was the power of correlative data that exposed the fact that she was pregnant. In this situation, Target used its vast data reserves, collected whenever a customer takes any action in the store (redeems a coupon, buys things, returns things, and so on) along with data it purchased from third-party brokers to build a profile about the store's shoppers. In this case, Target's data mining team was able to construct a model that correlated purchases of unscented lotion, oversized purses, and nutrition supplements with pregnancy. And indeed, this girl bought a bunch of those items, which led Target to conclude that she was pregnant before her father knew.

Notwithstanding the privacy challenges, there are those who say that, though we will have increasing access to data, there will still be a vast gap between those who have access and those who can derive meaning from the data. Remember, it's one thing to have data and quite another to be able to do something with it. The increasing volume of data being generated by our billions of connected devices and activities will make it challenging for the average consumer to make sense of the noise: and those with access to massive computational fabrics will have an inherent advantage (even if they don't know how to leverage it just yet).

I predict the rise of entire industries devoted to giving consumers better access to insights from public and personal data. And I suspect that equalizers will pop up; harkening back to our discussion of Wolfram Alpha's computational language and companies like Ayasdi, you see how ordinary users can write fairly simple natural language queries to derive insights that previously would have been the province of information scientists. As initiatives like the Wolfram Connected Devices Project become more fully realized, the data we collect will become even more powerful. For example, imagine that a small business owner could correlate foot traffic outside her shop with certain weather conditions. Maybe when it rains there is a fourfold increase in the number of people who pass by the shop on their way to a mall. How could the owner use this data to make better decisions about promotions and signage? Today, this would be a nearly impossible task for those without access to major sources of data and computational clusters; in a couple of years, this kind of information will be pedestrian.

A reduction in information asymmetry has the potential to radically boost our ability to live fuller, more productive lives, and a nice side effect of this data explosion is an increase in serendipity and opportunity, which comes when systems expose the hidden links between people and facts that were previously available only to the well connected.

Inome is a company in Seattle that finds these informational needles in haystacks. By combing through online data, the company finds the hidden links between people. Many of us in business know that our network is often the most powerful thing we have to work with. The problem is that not everyone has an influential network. In other words, I might be able to get my daughter into a great school, not just on her merits but because I happen to know a trustee. Is it fair? No. Does it happen every day? Definitely. Inome seeks to help people discover latent networks by exposing the links through other people they know, links that they didn't even know existed. By exploring these hidden connections, people have a better chance of finding the right person to reach out to for help, advice, or other connections. Companies like Inome are tapping into the more capable web to bring the power of connected data to everyone, radically enhancing the level of information *symmetry* in our society.

Societal Implications

Access to data, knowledge, and wisdom has a benefit that goes beyond making our own lives better. When the world has access to systems that can assess and compute a nearly infinite amount of data that is grounded in reality rather than bluster or fear, societies can make better decisions for their long-term prosperity.

Rationality Pervades

In addition to making our individual work and daily tasks more efficient, the new search systems could help free society from the tasks that consume so much of its time, yield poor decisions, and generally produce long-term outcomes that were unanticipated and often negative. Recall the "debates" we see in government on everything from environmental questions to immigration, natural resource exploration to health care—can anyone say these are actually improving the long-term prosperity of the republic? There is a reason public approval rates for Congress have dipped to 7 percent as of June 2014; there is much heat without a lot of light.

Thinking back to earlier chapters, where we saw that actions can be modeled with some level of probability, we don't have to "imagine" something happening; we can assign a level of certainty of the outcome happening to it. Decisions about emotionally charged problems could move out of the realm of rhetoric and emotion and into the territory of probability. You can argue all day that man-made sources of CO_2 are not contributing to climate change, but the facts dictate that there is a probability that they are. Once the planet, everything on it, and everyone who inhabits it are modeled and interactions can be extrapolated, it becomes easier to identify a course of action that balances the chance of cataclysmic environmental change against dreadful economic impacts. Funding mass transit becomes an easier proposition because we'll understand the number of riders who use different routes and the impact that lighter volume on the roads has on traffic and pollution. Health policy gets much easier to form as models evolve for the best treatment for various health conditions and populations.

At the same time, consider the implications for our political climate of systems that accurately track real-time sentiment of the electorate. The loudest, fringe elements of both parties will be exposed as just that—noisy outliers. The true sentiment of the majority of Americans becomes more transparent and will drown out the squeaky wheels.

I am not naïve enough to believe that data and search systems solve all societal ills. Will the next generation of search curtail lobbying, tone down crazed media, stir from apathy many of our fellow citizens, and fix everything else wrong with our republic? No. But I do think it will be harder for intemperate forces to hold sway over our democracy (and other democracies) when something approximating the truth is laid bare.

Trust, Nudging, and Societal Goodness

As I have said before, we are entering a golden age of search that has the potential to generate the happiest, healthiest, and most productive epoch in human history. But this age will only dawn if we trust and take advantage of our hinge, offloading certain tasks and decisions to systems that are likely more competent than we are. That is why we must be able to trust the systems: habits are hard to change, and if we build systems that require behavioral change (like instructing people to ask more complex questions of search rather than typing in a few keywords), we will face the adoption curve challenge; some people will fully embrace the new way while others will lag behind. Not only will this slow the overall trajectory toward a more powerful search, it will increase the divide between haves (whose access to robust information is greater) and have-nots (whose access is limited).

Imagine competing for a job with a candidate who has access to real-time decision tools *and* who knows how to use them effectively. In order for search to become the underlying fabric of our lives, it needs to be woven into mundane tasks that we already do. And for that to happen, people need to be able to trust that the system is acting on their behalf in a manner likely to generate the best outcome in whatever time frame they desire.

So let's assume that we are able to better model the future and put in place safeguards to prevent as many unintended consequences as possible, and then look at what can be done. A practical example of this in use today is the practice of "nudging." Pioneered by Richard Thaler and Cass Sunstein in their 2008 book *Nudge*, the core theory is that inertia plays a huge role in human behavior, meaning we are substantially more likely to continue doing that which is easy, even if it isn't in our best interests. Thaler and Sunstein contend that one can design conditions in a way that nudges people in beneficial directions without restricting freedom of choice. In other words, people often neglect to take actions that may have small, short-term costs but can produce large, long-term gains. Clever behavioral scientists have constructed scenarios in which simplified decision making encourages better outcomes. For example, the U.K.'s Behavioural Insights Team, also known as the Nudge Unit, which was recently privatized to take better advantage of the group's research in nongovernmental applications, showed the positive effects of removing barriers to better behavior like auto-enrolling people in pension plans (rather than having the employees opt in).

Now combine the power of nudging with the power of the new search paradigm. What if search systems, with their knowledge of the world, of you, and of the options available, could nudge you to take actions that, while potentially not in your short-term best interest, could benefit you in the medium to long term? Let's take a simple example: food. Imagine that I'm sitting in a restaurant. My device knows where I am. It queries the search store to understand the location and the menu found on the restaurant's website. At the same time, it is analyzing the nutritional content of items on the menu, including breaking down the likely ingredients based on the item descriptions. It can do the former, of course, by simply analyzing the website content; the latter is accomplished by search's innate understanding of the world; it understands that a "hamburger" likely consists of beef, bread, and maybe some cheese and lettuce.

Nudging: removing barriers to decisions that are good in the long term.

Here is where it gets fun: my search agent knows a lot about me. In fact, I gave it access to my DNA profile, so it is able to understand my likely health risks based upon my genetics. As it turns out, I have a 1.57 times higher than average risk of developing gout. Because gout is heavily influenced by nongenetic factors (such as what I eat), search can easily scan both the known (nutritional content) and the surmised (menu item composition) offerings of the restaurant to nudge me in a particular direction. When I'm deciding between two equally delicious entrees, search could nudge me to the one that likely is better for me given my predisposition to gout.

Looking a little further into our crystal ball, imagine how the Internet of Things and an understanding of the individual could come together to curb tendencies like binge drinking. According to the Centers for Disease Control and Prevention, more than half the alcohol consumed by adults in the United States is in the form of binge drinks.[1] Nearly a quarter of a trillion dollars is expended per year in lost productivity, health care, and crime due to this pattern of excessive drinking.

One can imagine how a government—or even a private bar—could use the power of search to moderate drinking to avoid bad outcomes. Tomorrow's Fitbit bracelet will likely contain galvanic sensors (the cheap sensors used today to measure electrical activity in your body), which have been shown to be able to detect the presence of alcohol in the wearer. Or possibly the next generation of wearable goggles will have inward facing cameras (similar to the system in Mercedes-Benz cars that detects when you are getting sleepy at the wheel) that measure pupil dilation when you are out at the bar. Combine that detailed personal information with an intelligent ordering system in the bar; the system could act in various ways to curb drinking, including slowing service of subsequent drinks or increasing the prices of drinks as a person becomes increasingly intoxicated. In this case, the technology and the principle of nudging come together to create tangible societal and personal benefits.

Business Implications

In 1937, an economist named Ronald Coase asked some fundamental questions about the nature of a "firm." In essence, his question was: "Why do firms or enterprises arise?" If the market is truly efficient, and the market rewards producers who are the best at producing a particular good or service most cheaply, why would a business owner hire rather than contract out for a particular task?

The answer, of course, was that there were transaction costs associated with using the market. So even though there were highly efficient producers of widgets that could compete with your hired staff on efficiency and price, the work you would have to do to *find* them made bringing them in-house more efficient.

What if finding the contract workers or more efficient producers of a particular good or service was cheap? What if search costs for the pieces of your firm you have in-house today dropped to near zero? Possibly, lower cost for searching for these pieces would tip the balance away from corporations, which have all that talent in house (but whose utility is probably not being maximized). What if the entire world of enterprise was instead made up of loosely coupled people working together when needed to deliver a product or service?

Certainly, in the world we have described, where everything and everyone has a digital presence, finding a factory with excess capacity to do a run of your widget or an attorney who has an extra fifteen hours to handle a contract negotiation would be simple. Coase wasn't saying the search costs are the only reason to form a firm—trade secrets, bargaining costs, and policing of regulations are also valid reasons—but finding the right person or company to perform work seems to be a disproportionate driver of enterprise costs. I think search can change that.

Can search technologies promote better governance, more efficient (and happier) citizens, and enterprises that work more productively than they do today with less human capital and infrastructure? The potential is there. Mass digitization—the key to a more powerful search—is already being led by consumers, and there are business models that could encourage even finer resolution in a short period of time. Certainly, many consumers in developed markets are looking for ways to offload tasks from their already harried schedules to systems that can help them save time, be smarter, and generally maximize their waking hours.

Governance and nudging that gently bend society toward a more sustainable end game seem to be moving from idea to full practice in a few Western governments. As people everywhere begin to embrace the power of the hinge—and, of course, as we tackle the serious issues of privacy, safety, and viable business models—we as a society will be able to let go of our (fruitless) attempts to understand and control all variables in an increasingly connected and noisy world. Even if we don't end up with quite the technical utopia we envision, either because of failures in theory or practice, advancements in even one area will yield disproportionate benefit to many.

CONCLUSION

Searching the Future

Throughout the book, we've glimpsed the challenges of search, but we've also seen how connected devices, intelligent systems, and higher-fidelity descriptions of the real world can materially change the way we think, behave, and manage our lives.

We've seen how search can help people change their actions ever so slightly in a given situation through nudging and how it can make sure users never forget anything they need to remember through augmentation. Search is as profound a breakthrough as any technical marvel this century, and yet we are barely approaching its potential.

Part of the reason, as we've seen, is the financial reality of running such a search system. It's hugely expensive to build and operate something akin to the "oracle on high," so paying for it needs to take a prominent role in its development. Those financial constraints have slowed search's broader development, but we see glimmers of hope on the horizon through innovative ad models and direct payments.

Technically, search systems may also hit a limit if they become unable to keep up with the exponential increase in the amount of data they are facing, but many fortunes have been lost betting against Moore's Law. Even so, the realities of data deluge may also prove too strong to overcome. Data scientists routinely lambast such statements as "With enough data, you can predict anything" by noting that correlation isn't causation. Will the future of search be well served by following correlative models? Probably not, as we would likely modify actions that would have no effect on outcomes. But certainly, in this world of buzzy big data, having correlations as a starting point and to help validate assumptions can positively affect our search for truth using the scientific method.

But part of the reason is that people aren't sure they want this future of smarter machines making us humans better; and this is not without cause. The revelations of the NSA's spying program and the amount of data being collected by both state and nonstate actors have given many people pause, and citizens are more fully considering the significance of their digital selves. Today, the serious conversations about privacy and security are mostly limited to those who work in the digital world, but as we continue to see breaches and mining of data for both legitimate and nefarious purposes, concern will likely spread.

In some ways, however, more personal data can prevent bad derived assumptions or outcomes. For example, a simple correlation routine that shows I made a call to a particular number in Pakistan and my frequent trips to the Middle East may trigger an "agency" to believe I am doing something they would rather I not do. However, more data would allow law enforcement to see that I was simply talking to a friend and we called his mom at home in Lahore to wish her a happy birthday; they'd know that I travel to the Middle East to visit my company's development centers.

There are concerns in addition to violations of privacy. Some critics, like Eli Pariser in his book *The Filter Bubble,* see the introduction of hyper-personalized and intelligent agents as a danger to discourse and a threat to an informed population, as people are exposed only to that information they are likely to want to see. There is still a lack of trust in the systems, a skepticism of mechanisms that are too massive to be seen and in many cases too massive to comprehend.

Me, I'm a techno-optimist. I see search and the systems that power it removing disability; I consider advances like those that helped Hugh Herr, who has replaced both his amputated legs with something that in many ways beats their biological equivalents as he competes in rock-climbing ascents at elite levels. I have seen Herr—who is head of the Biomechatronics research group at the MIT Media Lab—use data and sensors to replace the leg of a dancer who was injured in the Boston Marathon bombing and who now can continue her dance career.

I foresee people with dementia or Alzheimer's being helped with augmentations delivered through devices and systems that can replace some of what they have lost—like memory of where they put something and recognition of loved ones, which could be aided by devices like Google Glass. I see people who can spend more time with loved ones rather than stuck in traffic, burdened with a bad commute decision that takes that time away. Search, in my opinion, will be the backbone of a more engaged, happier, and more efficient society because it will remove barriers, guiding us to the most efficient course of action and enabling a transparency within society that will redefine the way we think about and treat one another.

Will there be bad actors who misuse the power granted by these systems? Yes. Will there be breaches that expose far too much information? Yes. Will the bad guys often outpace the good guys in the short term? Likely. It has happened with both the web and within search. With search, in particular, there were many ploys used by unscrupulous people to fool engines into showing their sites, often to trick users into clicking on an ad or signing up for a service. Today, more sophisticated attacks—from phishing scams to fake sites that infect people's machines with malware—occur daily, with the aim of getting people to divulge personal information for a variety of reasons.

But I also see the indefatigable human spirit overrun these bad actors. In 2011, when the Egyptian government shut off mobile phone and Internet access to prevent protestors from coordinating, people across Europe used fax machines to send old-fashioned dial-up modem numbers that protestors could use to communicate. Humans are like water: we are nature embodied. As the late futurist and author Michael Crichton said, we will always find a way.

In the end, we need to embrace the messiness, the complexity, and, let's face it, the unknowns that the future of the web and search hold. We should strive to understand both the potential and the risks of every new service, even if we don't fully realize the compound implications of these services becoming smarter and more connected. While there will certainly be outcomes we didn't anticipate—including a number of negative ones—the opportunities that a more connected, well-described, and eminently searchable society will bring makes improving search a worthy endeavor.

Throughout history, major advances have come when people embraced the unknown, whether that was Dr. Salk testing polio vaccine on himself or brave astronauts venturing into the void to further our understanding of our planet and our universe. Once we free ourselves from the strictures of what is possible today and let our minds wander and wonder about the recombinant powers of our technical marvels, I believe we as humans will truly advance to a higher plane, living better than we thought possible and questioning how we ever thrived without the power within us exposed by our machine assistants.

Bring on the hinge.

NOTES

Chapter 1

1. Statistics from Matthew Gray, "Web Growth Summary," 1996, accessed March 14, 2014, http://www.mit.edu/people/mkgray/net/web-growth-summary.html.
2. Jack Clark, "If This Doesn't Terrify You... Google's Computers OUTWIT Their Humans," *The Register,* November, 15, 2013, accessed February 10, 2014, http://www.theregister.co.uk/2013/11/15/google_thinking_machines/.
3. Larry Heck, "The Conversational Web," Microsoft Research, December 2012, accessed February 10, 2014, http://research.microsoft.com/pubs/193045/conversational-web.pdf, 40.
4. My friends in computer science will balk at this simplification. They will tell me, "Cats are indeed not generally alive, and in fact there are more dead cats than alive cats throughout history," and they are right. For each characteristic, there is a drill-down that is possible. Much like Isaac Asimov's three rules of robots, there will likely be some sort of moral code written into the systems that favors life over death. But in any case, building a set of models to determine why one shouldn't put a cat in a shredder is more complex and detailed than can be described in a book for readers who want to learn about the future of search without getting a PhD from Carnegie Mellon.

Chapter 4

1. Yarden Katz, "Noam Chomsky on Where Artificial Intelligence Went Wrong," November 1, 2012, accessed February 10, 2014, http://www.theatlantic.com/technology/archive/2012/11/noam-chomsky-on-where-artificial-intelligence-went-wrong/261637/.
2. Vikas Ashok, Song Feng, and Yejin Choi, "Success with Style: Using Writing Style to Predict Success of Novels," *Proceedings of the 2013 Conference on Empirical Methods in Natural Language Processing,* October 18-21, 2013, Seattle, WA, http://anthology.aclweb.org//D/D13/D13-1181.pdf, 1756.
3. Erik Sofge, "The End of Anonymity," *Popular Science,* January 15, 2014, accessed March 9, 2014, http://www.popsci.com/article/technology/end-anonymity?dom=PSC&loc=recent&lnk=1&con=the-end-of-anonymity.

Chapter 5

1. Ece Kamar and Eric Horvitz, "Jogger: Models for Context-Sensitive Reminding," *Proceedings of 10th International Conference on Autonomous Agents and Multiagent Systems* (AAMAS 2011), edited by Kagan Tumer, Pinar Yolum, Liz Sonenberg, and Peter Stone, May 2–6, 2011, Taipei, Taiwan, 17.
2. Tom Simonite, "Microsoft Builds a Browser for Your Past," *MIT Technology Review,* March 15, 2012, accessed March 17, 2014, http://www.technologyreview.com/news/427233/microsoft-builds-a-browser-for-your-past/page/2/.

Chapter 6

1. Barnaby Jack, "'Broken Hearts': How Plausible Was the Homeland Pacemaker Hack?," IO Active Labs Research, February 25, 2013, accessed March 17, 2014, http://blog.ioactive.com/2013/02/broken-hearts-how-plausible-was.html.
2. Alana Abramson, "Baby Monitor Hacking Alarms Houston Parents," ABC News, August 13, 2013, accessed March 17, 2014, http://abcnews.go.com/blogs/headlines/2013/08/baby-monitor-hacking-alarms-houston-parents/.
3. Bruce Schneier, "The Internet of Things Is Wildly Insecure—And Often Unpatchable," *Schneier on Security,* January 6, 2014, accessed February 12, 2014, https://www.schneier.com/essays/archives/2014/01/the_internet_of_thin.html.
4. Schneier, "The Internet of Things Is Wildly Insecure."
5. "On Hacking MicroSD Cards," *Bunnie: Studios,* December 29, 2013, accessed March 18, 2014, http://www.bunniestudios.com/blog/?p=3554.
6. danah boyd and Kate Crawford, *"Six Provocations for Big Data,"* paper presented at the *Oxford Internet Institute Decade in Internet Time Symposium*, September 22, 2011, http://ssrn.com/abstract=1926431, 6.
7. Anthony Bastardi and Eldar Shafir, "On the Pursuit and Misuse of Useless Information," *Journal of Personality and Social Psychology,* Vol. 75, No. 1 (1998): 22, http://psych.princeton.edu/psychology/research/shafir/pubs/Pursuit%20&%20Misuse%20Useless%20Info.pdf, 22.
8. Derrick Harris, "Has Ayasdi Turned Machine Learning into a Magic Bullet?," Gigaom, January 16, 2013, accessed March 20, 2014, http://gigaom.com/2013/01/16/has-ayasdi-turned-machine-learning-into-a-magic-bullet/.

Chapter 8

1. "Drinking in America: Myths, Realities, and Prevention Policy," Office of Juvenile Justice and Delinquency Prevention, Washington, DC, U.S. Department of Justice, Office of Justice Programs, 2005, http://www.udetc.org/documents/Drinking_in_America.pdf.

REFERENCES

Abramson, Alana. "Baby Monitor Hacking Alarms Houston Parents." *ABC News*, August 13, 2013. Accessed March 17, 2014. http://abcnews.go.com/blogs/headlines/2013/08/baby-monitor-hacking-alarms-houston-parents/.

Ashok, Vikas, Song Feng, and Yejin Choi. "Success with Style: Using Writing Style to Predict Success of Novels." Proceedings of the 2013 Conference on Empirical Methods in Natural Language Processing, Seattle, WA, October 18–21, 2013. http://anthology.aclweb.org//D/D13/D13-1181.pdf.

Bastardi, Anthony, and Eldar Shafir. "On the Pursuit and Misuse of Useless Information." *Journal of Personality and Social Psychology*, Vol. 75, No. 1 (1998): 22. http://psych.princeton.edu/psychology/research/shafir/pubs/Pursuit%20&%20Misuse%20Useless%20Info.pdf.

boyd, danah, and Kate Crawford. "Six Provocations for Big Data." Paper presented at the Oxford Internet Institute Decade in Internet Time Symposium, September 22, 2011, Oxford, UK. http://ssrn.com/abstract=1926431.

Clark, Jack. "If This Doesn't Terrify You . . . Google's Computers OUT-WIT Their Humans." *The Register*, November, 15, 2013. Accessed February 10, 2014. http://www.theregister.co.uk/2013/11/15/google_thinking_machines/.

"Drinking in America: Myths, Realities, and Prevention Policy." The Underage Drinking Enforcement Training Center, Office of Juvenile Justice and Delinquency Prevention, Department of Justice, Office of Justice Programs, 2005. http://www.udetc.org/documents/Drinking_in_America.pdf.

Gray, Matthew. "Web Growth Summary." 1996. Accessed March 14, 2014. http://www.mit.edu/people/mkgray/net/web-growth-summary.html.

Harris, Derrick. "Has Ayasdi Turned Machine Learning into a Magic Bullet?" *Gigaom*, January 16, 2013. Accessed March 20, 2014. http://gigaom.com/2013/01/16/has-ayasdi-turned-machine-learning-into-a-magic-bullet/.

Heck, Larry. "The Conversational Web." Microsoft Research. Accessed February 10, 2014. http://research.microsoft.com/pubs/193045/conversational-web.pdf.

Jack, Barnaby. "'Broken Hearts': How Plausible Was the Homeland Pacemaker Hack?" *IO Active Labs Research* blog, February 25, 2013.

Accessed March 17, 2014. http://blog.ioactive.com/2013/02/broken -hearts-how-plausible-was.html.

Kamar, Ece, and Eric Horvitz. "Jogger: Models for Context-Sensitive Reminding." Proceedings of 10th International Conference on Autonomous Agents and Multiagent Systems (AAMAS 2011), Taipei, Taiwan, May 2–6, 2011. Edited by Kagan Tumer, Pinar Yolum, Liz Sonenberg, and Peter Stone.

Katz, Yarden. "Noam Chomsky on Where Artificial Intelligence Went Wrong." *The Atlantic*, November 1, 2012. Accessed February 10, 2014. http://www.theatlantic.com/technology/archive/2012/11/noam -chomsky-on-where-artificial-intelligence-went-wrong/261637/.

"On Hacking MicroSD Cards." *Bunnie: Studios*, December 29, 2013. Accessed March 18, 2014. http://www.bunniestudios.com/ blog/?p=3554.

Schneier, Bruce. "The Internet of Things Is Wildly Insecure—And Often Unpatchable." *Schneier on Security*, January 6, 2014. Accessed February 12, 2014. http://www.schneier.com/essays/archives/2014/01/the _internet_of_thin.html.

Simonite, Tom. "Microsoft Builds a Browser for Your Past." *MIT Technology Review*, March 15, 2012. Accessed March 17, 2014. http://www.technologyreview.com/news/427233/microsoft-builds –a–browser-for-your-past/page/2/.

Sofge, Erik. "The End of Anonymity," *Popular Science*, January 15, 2014. Accessed March 9, 2014. http://www.popsci.com/article/ technology/end-anonymity?dom=PSC&loc=recent&lnk=1&con =the-end–of–anonymity.

INDEX

A

A/B testing, 170
access to data, technology challenges, 115–116
action-based web, 72–73
advertising
  business model challenges, 138–143
  cross-sided networks, 144
  diversification of revenue streams, 144
  free services, 144–145
  notion of micropayments, 140
  problem of attribution, 139
  rapid advancement in search, 140
  retargeting, 139
Age of Context (Scoble and Israel), 106
AI (artificial intelligence), 85
AllJoyn system, 75–76
analog rationality, 85
anchor text, history of modern search, 4
Anderson, Chris, 26
Animetrics, 92
apps
  "action" portion of, 68–69
  action-based web, 72–73
  explosion of, 66–67
  micropayment, 69–70
  persistent login and accounts, 70
  ratings, 70
  registration of capabilities, 69
Arduino, 74
artificial intelligence (AI), 85
authentication mechanisms, 118
authoritative systems, 92
authority, unclear, 84–85
Autographer, 15
Ayasdi, 133–135

B

Bastardi, Anthony, 133
Berners-Lee, Tim, 2
Beyond Verbal, 88
bias-variance tradeoff, 101–102
Bing entity repository, 57
biofeedback sensors, 168
blind curiosity, 63–64
BlueKai, 148–149
Borel, Emile, 1
brain
  brain imaging, 39–40
  mimicking the, 93–94
  search systems working like the, 41
brain imaging, 39–40
breaking news stories, 112
Brin, Sergey, 4
business implications, value of sharing data, 183–184
business model challenges, what holds us back
  advertising, 138–143
  data use issues, 158–159
  diversification of revenue streams, 144
  personal clouds, 154–155
  personal dimensions, 147–148
  personal rights, 155–157
  privacy, 145–154
  revenue generation, 137–138
  social dimensions, 147–148
  societal dimensions, 147–148
  technical dimensions, 147–148
  terms of servitude, 155–157

C

CAD systems, 23
capable web, 8–9
  connected reality, 12
  devices, 15–16

capable web (*cont.*)
  events, 17–18
  Facebook, 10–11
  fueled by devices, 22–26
  fueled by ubiquitous communication,
    26–28
  hybrid systems, 18–19
  "Internet of Things," 16–17
  payment systems, 19–20
  personal information, 12
  physical world with, 29–31
  sensors, 20–22
  services, 12–15
  Twitter, 10
  video, 10
cataloging, history of modern search, 3
causation, 63–64
chemical sampling devices, 168
Chomsky, Noam, 85
Coase, Ronald, 183
Commotion, 28
competition in search, 77–78
conformity and decision paralysis,
    131–133
connected reality, 12
connections, World Wide Web
    evolution, 2
Conrad, Jeremy, 23, 169
consumers, digitizing by, 167–169
control loop, 169–171
conversation, listening devices, 167
conversational understanding, 47–48
correlation and causation, 63–64
Cortana, 98
curiosity, 63–64

D
DARPA Network Challenge, 95
data mining, technology challenges,
    126
data profiles, technology challenges,
    116
data storage, technology challenges,
    122–124
data use issues, business model
    challenges, 158–159
data, World Wide Web evolution, 2
Davis, Marc, 77, 110–111, 145
decision making, real-time, 111–113
decision paralysis and conformity,
    131–133

deep neural networks (DNNs), 44
devices
  and capable web, 15–16
  device-level intelligence, 103–104
  as influencer, 75–77
  self controlled, 76
digitizing
  by consumers and citizens, 167–169
  embracing complexity of digital self,
    161–165
  by producers, 165–167
disk space, technology challenges, 126
diversification of revenue streams, 144
DNNs (deep neural networks), 44
Dropbox, 145
Dropcam, 10
Dumais, Susan, 96, 99, 107–108

E
efficiency, 172–173
emotional decision making, 88
energy management, 124
"entity understanding," 42
Epstein, Robert, 132
error, 100–102
Estimote, 104
Eventbrite, 17
events, and capable web, 17–18
EverythingMe, 72
evolution of the web, 1–3
experience-based techniques
    (heuristics), 78–79
eye tracking, 108–109

F
face recognition, 92
Facebook
  and capable web, 10–12
  likes, 11
  personal information in, 12
Facebook Login, 117
facial recognition software, 10
failed search queries, 52
FanFootage, 19
FARG (Fluid Analogies Research
    Group), 93
fault measurement, 169
fidelity of measurements, 86
FieldTripper app, 106
Filter Bubble, The (Pariser), 132
FireHost, 154

fitness tracking, 162
Fluid Analogies Research Group
    (FARG), 93
food sampling devices, 168
Foodspotting, 19
Friendster, 127
*From X-Rays to Silly Putty via Uranus:
    Serendipity and Its Role in Web
    Search,* 132
future intents, 110–111
future of search, 185–188

G
GateGuru, connection of virtual events
    to physical applications, 14
genetics, 89
genomics, 87
Gesture, 49
Google Glass, 10, 15–16, 106
Google Knowledge Graph, 57
Google Now, 45
GoPro, 10
graphs
    illustration of set of, 33
    social, 32–33
    understanding of objects from
        infinite set of angles, 33–36

H
happiness
    efficiency as key to, 172–173
    question of next-generation search
        increasing, 78–81
hardware design cots, 23–25
hardware, license-free platforms, 119
heuristics (experience-based
    techniques), 78–79
hierarchical index, 3
history of modern search, 3–5
Hofstadter, Douglas, 93–94
home energy management, 124–125
Horvitz, Eric, 60–61, 63, 100, 109
Huang, Andrew, 121–122
human conversation refinement, 47
humanity
    lack of, 84
    modeling of, 93
    superhuman, 113–114
Humin app, 111
hybrid systems and capable web, 18–19
hypertext documents, 1–2

I
IBM's Watson, 91, 123
IFTTT (If This, Then That), 13–14
image search, history of modern search, 6
images and capable web, 9–10
impedance mismatch, 84
inattentional blindness, 30
index, history of modern search, 3–4
information asymmetry reduction,
    173–176
Inome company, 177
input, World Wide Web evolution, 2
INRIX, connection of virtual events to
    physical applications, 13
Insight Discovery Platform service, 133
insights through curiosity, 63–65
"Internet of Things," 16–17
introduction of action, 42
iPhone app, 88
Israel, Shel
    Age of Context, 106
Ivee hardware assistant, 50

J
"just-in-time information," 106

K
Kahneman, Daniel, 79–80
keyword search, 77
Kickstarter, 25
Kinect sensors, 105
Knowledge Graph, Google, 57
known knowns, 80
known unknowns, 80
known-item search, 38–39
Koemei system, 10
Koul, Anirudh, 112, 123–124, 126
Kurzweil, Ray, 39–40, 93

L
lack of humanity, 84
language challenges
    conversational understanding, 47–48
    speech recognition, 45
language-based descriptions, 5–8
Law, Edith, 94–95
license-free hardware platforms, 119
Lifebrowser, 109–110
LifeCam, 15
likes, Facebook, 11
LinkedIn, 12

listening devices, 167
Livshits, Ben, 148–150
Local Scout, 98
location-based alerts, 104
login, persistent login and accounts,
    70

M
machine learning, 89–92
magnetometers, 16
Marchese, Joe, 141–142
matching requests, blend of signals and
    knowledge which search engine
    has access, 43
Mechanical Turk, 83–84
Meetup, 17
memorization, 107–110
memory cards, 121
microcomputers, technology
    challenges, 121–122
micropayments, 69–70
Microsoft MAVIS system, 10
Microsoft Xbox One, 105
mobile devices, abilities to augment
    search as immediately needed,
    53–54
modems, World Wide Wed evolution,
    2
modern search, history of, 3–5
MOOC (Massive Open Online
    Courses), 23
Moto X, 49
multitasking, balancing with attention
    and memory, 110
Music Genome Project, 89–90

N
Nanosatisfi, 23
news stories, 112
noise level sensors, 168
non-instrumental information,
    technology challenges, 133
nudging, 180–182

O
object features and pattern recognition,
    31–32
Oculus Rift, 106
OpenTable, 13
ownership of data, technology
    challenges, 115–116

P
Page, Larry, 4
Pandora, 91, 141
Paradox of Choice, The (Schwartz),
    79, 133
Pariser, Eli
    The Filter Bubble, 132
PARLANCE project, 45–46
pattern recognition, 29–31
payment systems
    and capable web, 19–20
    micropayments, 69–70
PayPal, 19
personal clouds, business model
    challenges, 154–155
personal dimensions, business model
    challenges, 147–148
personal implications, value of sharing
    data, 171
personal information
    and capable web, 12
    in LinkedIn and Facebook, 12
    and technology challenges, 116
personal rights, business model
    challenges, 155–157
personal tracking devices, 16–17
Peto, Richard, 101
phone number search, 92
phrasing in search queries, 51
picocells, 27–28
Postmates, 13
predictive search, 59–62, 65
privacy, business model challenges,
    145–154
PrivacyFix, 149
producers, digitizing by, 165–167
Project Louise, 106

Q
Quixey, 72

R
Rackspace, 154
radio innovations, 27–28
Raspberry Pi, 73–74
ratings, 70
rationality
    challenges of gapping bridge between
        machine and human abilities, 85
    societal implications, 178–179
Ready the Hand notion, 77

RealNetworks, 10
real-time decision making, 111–113
real-time transcription, 16
recipe analysis, 91–92
recognizers, brain imaging, 40
references, 191–192
Refresh app, 111
RePriv system, 150–152
resolution inputs, 87–88
revenue generation, business model
    challenges, 137–138
rights, business model challenges,
    155–157
Robertson, Ronald, 132
rule-based systems
    and PARLANCE project, 45–46
    speech recognition, 44–45

S
Schneier, Bruce, 120–121
Schwartz, Barry, 79, 133
Scoble, Robert
    Age of Context, 106
Seamless, 14
search engines
    history of modern search, 4
    people as, 94–96
search queries
    abilities to augment search as
        immediately needed, 53–54
    blend of signals and knowledge
        which search engine has access,
        43
    challenges of phrasing, 51
    and "entity understanding," 42
    failed, 52
    formulation challenges, 51–52
    history of modern search, 4
    next generation of search, 38–39,
        43–44
    time-sensitive, 60
SeatGeek, 14
security, technology challenges,
    119–122
self controlled devices, 76
sensors
    and capable web, 20–22
    location-based alerts, 104
Serval Project, 28
services
    and capable web, 12–15

explosion of virtual event
    connections to physical
    applications, 13–15
servitude, business model challenges,
    155–157
shared data, technology challenges,
    117–119
Shirky, Clay, 173
Siri
    and action-based web, 72–73
    speech recognition and language
        challenges, 45
SkyNet, 76
slow search, 96–100
SmartThings, 14
social dimensions, business model
    challenges, 147–148
social graph, 32–33
social networks and capable web, 10
societal dimensions
    business model challenges, 147–148
    value of sharing data, 178–182
societal goodness, 180–182
speech recognition
    conversational understanding, 47–49
    language challenges, 45
    machine learning advances, 89
    rule-based systems, 44–45
speed of search, 96–100
speed tracking sensors, 168
SpotHero, 13
Spotify, 141
Square, 19
statistical representations, technology
    challenges, 127
stimulus
    acting in way of what is in line with
        user's goals, 44
    blend of signals and knowledge
        which search engine has access, 43
    change in state concept, 43
subsegments, 101
Sunstein, Cass, 180–181
systems biology, 87

T
"tail answers," 99
Target, 60
TaskRabbit, 12
technical dimensions, business model
    challenges, 147–148

technology challenges, what holds
search back
access to and ownership of data,
115–117
data mining, 126
data storage, 122–124
decision paralysis and conformity,
131–133
disk space, 126
energy management, 124
memory cards, 121
microcomputers, 121–122
non-instrumental information, 133
security, 119–122
statistical representations, 127
unintended outcomes, 128–129, 131,
133
USB devices, 121
tethering, 27
Thaler, Richard, 180–181
time-sensitive queries, 60
Tonido, 154
TOSDR.org, 155–156
tracking devices, 16–17
training data, 89
transcription, real-time, 16
transparency, and unintended
outcomes, 130
TrueVault, 141
trust, 180–182
Turing Test, 84
Twitter, 10

U
Uber, connection of virtual events to
physical applications, 14
UDDI (Universal Description Discovery
and Integration), 69
unclear authority, 84–85
unintended outcomes, technology
challenges, 128–129, 131, 133
Universal Description Discovery and
Integration (UDDI), 69
unknown unknowns, 80
USB devices, 121

V
value of sharing data
business implications, 183–184

control loop, 169–171
digitizing by consumers and citizens,
167–169
digitizing by producers, 165–167
embracing complexity of digital self,
161–165
equalized access to knowledge,
173–176
implications on life, 171
information asymmetry reduction,
173–177
personal implications, 171
societal implications, 178–182
trust, nudging, and societal
goodness, 180–182
VeriFone, 19
video search
and capable web, 10
history of modern search,
6–7
visual capturing, 167–168

W
Watson, IBM, 91, 123
Waze, 13, 113
web, evolution of, 1–3
Westergren, Tim, 89
Whitehead, Alfred North,
81
Windows Phone, 73, 98
Wolfram Alpha, 54–55, 57,
73–74
Wolfram Connected Devices, 54
Wolfram Language, 54–55
World Economic Forum's Rethinking
Personal Data Project, 155–156
World Wide Web, evolution of, 1–3
WYSIATI (What You *See* Is All There
Is) concept, 80

X
Xbox One (Microsoft), 105

Y
Yelp, 17
YouTube, 10

Z
Zemanta, 107

ABOUT THE AUTHOR

Stefan Weitz is a Senior Director of Search at Microsoft and charged with working with people and organizations across the industry to promote and improve Search technologies. While focused on Microsoft's product line, he works across the industry to understand searcher behavior, academic developments, and innovations from all over and, in his role as an evangelist for Search, gathers and distills feedback to drive fundamental search improvements.

Prior to Search, Stefan led the strategy to develop Microsoft's next generation online platforms and developed Microsoft's muni WiFi strategy and implementation, leading the charge to blanket free WiFi access across metropolitan cities. Stefan has been writing code since he was 8 years old and is fluent in both hardware and software architecture, trends, and potentials. A 17-year Microsoft veteran, he has led various groups in Windows, hardware, Informatics Security, and global business strategy in roles ranging from development to program management, business development to marketing. Stefan holds a half-dozen patents in various disciplines and is a frequent lecturer to industry and academic groups on the future of information storage, retrieval, and usage.

Stefan is a huge gadget 'junkie' and can often be found in electronics shops across the world looking for the elusive perfect piece of tech. Stefan also serves on advisory boards for many startups ranging from biometrics to advertising to virtualization and is an active Angel investor. In his spare cycles, he is working with national educational reinvention groups to reboot K-12 education in this country and is actively advising startups that are focusing on boosting student achievement through technology and big data. He is on the GenCon Board for Conservation International and active in Endeavor Global, a non-profit dedicated to incubating high-impact startups in developing markets. Finally, Stefan is working on a book with the nation's youngest VC to promote entrepreneurism to the young people of our planet.

He lives in Seattle, WA.